Creating Book Clubs in the English Language Classroom

I0890414

Creating Book Clubs in the English Language Classroom

A Model for Teachers of Adults

Barbara Vaille and
Jennifer QuinnWilliams

Copyright © by the University of Michigan 2006
All rights reserved
ISBN 0-472-03109-0
Published in the United States of America
The University of Michigan Press
Manufactured in the United States of America

∞ Printed on acid-free paper

2009 2008 2007 2006 4 3 2 1

No part of this publication may be reproduced, stored in a retrieval system, or transmitted in any form or by any means, electronic, mechanical, or otherwise, without the written permission of the publisher.

Contents

To the Teacher

WE love to teach. Teaching is our vocation and our avocation. It's our volunteer work and our profession. We also love to read. We love to talk to each other about what we've read. It seems we are always saying, "I read the best book!" We share the ideas, connections to our lives, and lessons we've learned from the many wonderful tales we've read.

We recognized that these passions were not mutually exclusive in a seminar we attended with Stephen Krashen in 1998, in Denver, Colorado. We had registered for the seminar because we wanted to include more reading in our Adult English Language Learners (ELL) program, to know what kind of reading to include and, also, to learn about the research. Krashen advocated "reading for pleasure" as part of a good ELL program, citing a 1994 study (Cho and Krashen) that appears to have found that Korean women who read the *Sweet Valley High* series for teens showed marked improvement in their speaking vocabularies and in spoken English in general. Of course, these were our goals too.

Studies indicate that ELL students in high-level academic settings, such as universities, show improvement on test scores and reading comprehension when provided with ample reading material and time (Mason and Krashen 1997; Lao and Krashen 2000). In the Lao and Krashen study (2000), students in a popular literature course who read for content and enjoyment, also felt that "what they had learned in the course would help them in other university courses" (Krashen 2003). Intuitively, we were sure this was true, so we vowed—somehow—to find a way to incorporate reading for pleasure into our schedule. But that wasn't all. We wanted our students to talk to each other about what they were reading, and the idea of a class book club was born.

Reading for pleasure in our class involves providing students with a variety of high-interest materials to read and giving them plenty of time in class to do the reading. While the students are reading, we are also reading, often some of the same materials they are, but sometimes other books or articles.

Like Krashen, we also want to provide *comprehensible input* (understandable messages) through reading. When we introduce students to the structure of the book club, we instructors provide comprehensible input for our students by reading and pondering out loud. This thinking out loud helps students understand *how* to read (Keene and Zimmerman 1997). The book club discussions also help our students negotiate meaning, which is an important way to use their new vocabulary and share connections about the text.

If you've picked up this book, perhaps it's because you, too, are a teacher who wants to make some changes in the reading component of your curriculum. You might already know that reading is one of the best ways to improve English acquisition and would like to add more of it to your program, but you aren't sure how to do it. This book can help—it provides a model for adding more reading through implementation of a book club in your classroom.

As the co-directors and teachers of the AIMS (Authentic Immersion Multilevel Systems) Adult ELL Program of Dora Moore K–8 School, we offer beginning and multilevel classes for community members and parents of children at this Denver public school. (For the sake of clarity *we* is used in the book to indicate that we both teach the multilevel class; however, there is only one instructor teaching at any given time.) We use communicative methods to teach English through content and have developed AIMS to assist our students in acquiring English. All of our students are literate in their own language and can use the Roman alphabet, although education levels vary widely.

After our experience with Dr. Krashen, we embarked on a search for books that would be appropriate, interesting, and enjoyable for our students. We knew that student interest in the reading material was going to be key to our students wanting to read. When we couldn't find any that we thought they could love, we decided to write our own. We wrote a story about a young Mexican immigrant woman who learns to stand on her own feet in the United States after her husband abandons her and their small child. In *Flor's Journey to Independence,* we used simple English but did not control for grammar or vocabulary; we used the language that was necessary to tell a good story and still be authentic. We gave the story to our class to read, and the students not only enjoyed it, they loved it! Although we knew they liked the story, the discussions that followed were disappointing. They were mostly retellings instead of making their own connections.

It was obvious that we needed some structure for the discussions. As you are undoubtedly aware, just asking students to "talk about it" does not work. Given our philosophy that students should help design the content of our classes, we did not want the discussions to be about topics we, the instructors, had assigned. We wanted to know how the students related to the story, what their experiences were, and why they found the book so entertaining and interesting.

Our book club model format evolved from our own experiences in developing book clubs (or discussion groups) for children, plus from many helpful books on book clubs and reading (see the Bibliography). We both had experience with Great Books and the concept of shared inquiry, where discussion leaders and participants work together, without lists of comprehension questions, to determine the importance of a story. Through Great

Books, we became familiar with the interpretive, or authentic, question, one to which the readers and the discussion leader do not know the answer, as opposed to a question that merely tests the reader's recall of actions and characters in the story. Answering an authentic question requires the use of background knowledge and inferences about the story.

For example, a question that tests recall from the fairy tale *Jack and the Beanstalk* might be: "What did Jack do when he saw that a beanstalk had grown outside his window?" The answer to this question is in the story: He climbed the beanstalk. An authentic question would be: "I wonder whether Jack climbed that beanstalk out of curiosity or fear." The answer to this question does not necessarily have a "right" answer and can start a thoughtful conversation including the follow-up question: "Why curiosity or fear?" The reader has to think not only about Jack's mother and how angry or disappointed she was with him for trading their cow for beans, but also about Jack's character, who has shown himself willing to believe in miracles (magic beans) and take chances (disobeying his mother by bringing back beans instead of gold or milk, or whatever item the story version specifies).

In addition, we had worked with children in book clubs, using the comprehension strategies identified by reading researchers to be the ones that proficient readers use (see Keene and Zimmerman 1997). In these book clubs, children make personal connections to the books and use images, predictions, questions, and inferences to help them analyze and evaluate (i.e., higher-order thinking skills) the literature they read. The children are taught each strategy discretely, so that eventually they will be synthesizing, which is changing their ideas and thinking as they read the story.

We had many long talks about how to get adult ELL students to be able to read and discuss *Flor* with the same enthusiasm and interest that the children in our book clubs had shown, and without relying on review and comprehension questions, vocabulary exercises, or grammar lessons. We wanted authentic conversation generated by the students. Then we had the *aha* moment: We realized that we could use the same comprehension strategies that we had used to guide children's book clubs with our adult students. And it worked!

In *The Book Club Connection: Literacy Learning and Classroom Talk*, Cynthia Brock (1997) cites Makhail Bakhtian: "Meaningful situated language facilitates learning." We've seen this in our book club. It provides the environment for adult learners to use their thoughts and feelings about works of literature as a basis for meaningful communication in a second (or third, or fourth) language.

Although we do rely heavily on some basic reading techniques from books written for teachers of elementary and secondary students, it's important to note that book clubs for children have a somewhat different focus than those for adults learning English. Book clubs for children have as their primary objective "creating an instructional environment in which students would develop the necessary literary knowledge and literacy tools to participate fully and effectively in talk about text" (McMahon et al. 1997). In contrast, our adults want to acquire proficiency in English. They come to us with rich life backgrounds and varying levels of educational accomplishment. While some hold advanced degrees, others in the same class might have a sixth-grade education. Our adult students may or may not be voracious native-language readers, but all of them can read, and most are already able to make connections to text in their own languages. Others, especially those with lower levels of education, will greatly benefit from learning how to use comprehension strategies to think and talk about what they read. Our main objective again, though, is to aid our students in acquiring English.

This said, the book clubs developed for children in elementary and secondary schools, with a little tweaking, provided excellent resources for us to set up a book club in our adult ELL classroom.

Our book club has three components: reading, discussion, and writing a Book Log entry. These parts, especially the discussion and Book Log portion, are described in detail in Chapters 3–9. During the discussion portion of the book club, our students negotiate meaning and engage in authentic discussion about "issues and ideas that they choose," (Brock 1997), rather than teacher-generated topics. The discussion portion is especially important because this is where students are free to experiment with language—something that three studies of book clubs of children acquiring second languages (Raphael and Brock 1993; Goatley et al. 1995; Brock 1995) have corroborated. These studies suggest that book clubs aid language acquisition. Over the four years that we have conducted book club in our multilevel class, we have certainly found this to be true for our adult students as well.

In summary, the primary goals of our book club are:

◊ to provide comprehensible input, through reading and discussion, for all students.
◊ to improve our students' English skills through reading.
◊ to give students opportunities to negotiate meaning and experiment with language.

In any book club or discussion group, the choice of books is important. You don't need to write your own story, as we did! In fact, we use children's books to introduce students to the book club because most of our students are also parents, and this is an excellent way to promote parental involvement in reading. As we move through the year with the book club, our students read both fiction and non-fiction (often in the form of newspaper and magazine articles) as reading choices. But, any quality, high-interest, enjoyable fiction or non-fiction can be used to achieve the main goals of a book club.

Some of the other advantages of using the book club model as presented here are:

- ◊ Students who are parents can help improve the literacy skills of their children.
- ◊ Parents are introduced to quality children's literature.
- ◊ Through our meaningful and interesting discussions, which expose students to a variety of cultural and personal perspectives, a sense of community is created in class.
- ◊ Students share knowledge and information about important topics, from basic life skills to the news of the day.

A Few Notes about the Contents of This Book

- Although we wrote this book with the adult ELL learner in mind, it can be adapted easily to Adult Basic Education (ABE) classroom situations. The same strategies will work for ABE and ELL students. ABE students will profit from learning some literacy tools useful for analysis and discussion of literature, and they will improve their reading. In fact, the same comprehension strategies work well in high school or even middle school. However, we would not recommend the use of our series of stories with these students because they were written for an adult audience.
- Although we sometimes ask our students to share, we try to have class sets of the books we use. Students read at dif-

ferent paces and often want to borrow books to take home, which we encourage if they belong to our program. Many booksellers offer discounts on class sets or multiple purchases, and local libraries often carry multiple copies. The kindergarten, first grade, and second grade teachers in our school share their multiple copies of children's books with us.

- We have used an anecdotal style in this book because we are modeling how a book club works. We present our own experiences with our students and examples of how the book club works in our program. When possible, we provide ideas for use in other types of adult programs.

A final note: If you read *Flor's Journey to Independence* before continuing with this book, our examples and explanations may be clearer. *Flor* may be purchased through our publisher, the University of Michigan Press. A modified (simpler version) of *Flor* is available at *www.press.umich.edu/esl/stories.*

—Barbara Vaille and Jennifer QuinnWilliams

Introduction: Why a Book Club?

IMAGINE your students, sitting in small groups of five or six, earnestly and eagerly holding a discussion in English. Imagine the topics being learner-generated and the discussion natural, without formal comprehension questions or post-reading exercises. In our book club, this is not just a glorious pipe dream—it's reality. We use a specific set of comprehension strategies to provide a framework for our beginning to advanced adult ELL students in our multilevel class. Once students know how to use these strategies, we let them take it from there. The result has been increased levels of reading for pleasure, wider vocabularies, and the practice of higher-order thinking skills, such as analyzing and evaluating stories and the ideas in them, in class discussions.

We have both anecdotal and test score results that bear out our contention that book club works. After 50 hours in our class, our students typically improve between one and two levels on the standardized test, the BEST Plus, a speaking and listening test that we use to measure growth. While all aspects of the class contribute to this growth, we feel certain that the book club is an important factor. Students tell us about other books they have read once they realize how enjoyable and helpful reading in English is. We see improvement in their daily interactive journal entries, with words popping up from stories we have read. For example, after several months of our book club, one student started to bring in newspaper articles (in her native language and English) to share during our Current Events session. She was reading these stories outside of class for enjoyment.

The books we provide for our students are high-interest pleasure books. High-interest books are important, whether you are using fiction or non-fiction, because reading in a second language is challenging, and students need to be motivated to move on in the story. If students want to know what happens next, or are fascinated by the material, they will make the extra effort required to keep reading and will learn to enjoy it. When one of our students initially resisted reading *Flor* because other students had summarized the beginning of the book for him and he thought it would be too sad, we asked him to read just one chapter. He did, but he didn't stop there. He read the entire book and then wrote us a beautiful essay on why reading in general is important and why *Flor,* specifically, is a good book. Once his interest was piqued, he couldn't put *Flor* down, even though his English was at a level that made the reading challenging for him.

Textbooks and readers with comprehension questions, grammar exercises, or vocabulary lessons may have their place in a curriculum, but they are not good choices for book clubs. Book club reading and discussions must focus on reading, on students making connections with what they are reading and generating ideas, and then discussing these ideas and connections. The emphasis is on comprehending the reading and being understood as they communicate their connections during discussion. The discussions are student-driven as opposed to text-driven. This fact helps students enjoy what they read because the focus isn't on understanding something to get a comprehension question correct, and there is less pressure to have "the right" ideas or answers. Students begin to look within themselves for ideas and begin to share them in a more natural way. Once lessons, exercises, and tests are introduced, they interfere with and dilute this process and the discussion is no longer about issues the students care about.

Based on the research of Graves (1991) and our own experience, the use of comprehension strategies helps learners "make sense of the world around them through reading." We've seen our book club help our adult students make sense of English and the new country in which they find themselves. And it all starts with reading.

Research

As we researched books that would be appropriate, interesting, and enjoyable reading for our students, we discovered that many other educators and researchers advocate reading for pleasure in both ABE and ELL classrooms. In an article in a Department of Education report titled *Focus on Basics*, J. Storey and T. Modleski are quoted as finding that reading for pleasure " 'provides a terrain on which to dream,' with fantasies that both reflect and counter 'the very real problems and tensions in [people's] lives.' " We believe this to be true for English language learners as well as native English speakers.

Perhaps the best evidence of this came from a student who wrote to us after reading *Flor:* "It describes with details for each part of the story. When I'm reading I can see in my mind all pictures in Flor's life. Is strange, but I feel very emotion in my heart because I'm very *sensible* (sensitive) and I feel happy and sad through the chapters. Maybe I have the opportunity to know many women who are living the same situation as Flor."

When students read for pleasure, it generates genuine discussion. They become excited about the conversations they are having and forget that English is challenging. During reading, they build on vocabulary they know and learn new vocabulary, often even determining possible meanings of words through the contexts of the passages. During discussion, they collaborate with other students to determine bigger meanings/themes in the story. They make connections between the book, themselves, their cultures, and the world. They become "members of the club" (Krashen 2003), building community as they participate in the exclusive world of English speakers.

For example, after reading the first chapter of the second story we wrote about a Turkish woman named Senem, our multilevel students shared their own stories. Many students were very sympathetic toward one woman who said she had a child as a compromise with her husband; like Senem, she wanted to continue her busy career. Another woman said she wanted three children, but wasn't strong enough to have more than two. This may seem like a conversation that is too personal for the classroom. Our students felt comfortable discussing it. However, only the teacher will know if her class can handle personal discussions. It's essential that teachers reinforce that students should not talk about anything that makes them uncomfortable, and that they can leave the classroom if someone else wants to discuss something they think is too personal.

We believe promoting this sense of community and fellowship in a book club aids in lowering the "affective filter," a block that Krashen hypothesizes keeps input from reaching Noam Chomsky's "language acquisition device" in the brain (Dulay, Burt, and Krashen 1982). Once the affective filters of our students are lowered, they are open to comprehensible input in our multilevel and beginner classes.

As previously discussed, research strongly supports reading for pleasure as a primary tool for improving reading comprehension, grammar, and passive and active vocabularies among primary and secondary school students (Nagy, Herman, and Anderson 1985; Anderson, Wilson, and Fielding 1988; Foertsch 1992).

This includes free voluntary reading (FVR) and sustained silent reading (SSR) (where students select their own reading material and read silently for a specified portion of each day or class period). In *The Power of Reading,* Krashen reviews the results of 41 studies of FVR, in which 38 supported the idea that this practice results in improved reading comprehension. In addition to the studies cited in *To the Teacher* (see p. x), two other studies of school-aged children learning English as a foreign language showed free voluntary or shared reading to be beneficial (Elley and Mangubhai 1983; Elley 1998). The students in these studies outperformed children being taught English by traditional methods in tests of reading comprehension, vocabulary, oral language, grammar, listening comprehension, and writing.

Although there are fewer studies advocating reading for pleasure as an important component of an adult ELL curriculum, at least three studies (Gradman and Hanania 1991; Mason and Krashen 1997; Lao and Krashen 2000) support reading for pleasure. The 1991 study showed that pleasure reading resulted in learning new words without "trying to" and also increased scores on the TOEFL® (paper-and-pencil test).

The comprehension strategies in our book club model are based on research performed in the 1980s on the cognitive strategies that proficient readers use to interpret what they read. This body of research has become known as the "proficient reader research" (Keene and Zimmerman 1997). It showed that proficient readers thought about their own thinking during reading and used a consistent set of seven or eight strategies while doing this thinking (Keene and Zimmerman 1997).

A book club of teachers formed by Colorado's Public Education Coalition (now Public Education Business Coalition, PEBC), of which Keene and Zimmerman are a part, realized that "by being metacognitive (literally to think about one's own thinking)—we could actually deepen and enhance our comprehension of the text." They then set out to study teachers across the country to see if the comprehension strategies were being systematically taught in classrooms to help children become better at thinking about their reading and therefore more proficient. They did not find any programs that were teaching children *how to comprehend,* which goes beyond knowing *how to read* (i.e., *decode*).

Since then, Ellin Oliver Keene, Susan Zimmerman, and other elementary and secondary educators have developed effective methods of introducing the strategies to improve students' comprehension. We have adapted these methodologies to our adult ELL classroom. These strategies are described in detail in Chapters 3–8.

Materials

Some educators have asked us whether adult students like the children's books. Yes! There is never as much laughter as when we are reading a funny picture book with detailed illustrations, such as *Guess What?* by Mem Fox. Whether the books are touching, sad, or educational, our students are fond of them. Who doesn't like to be read to now and then? Our students also enjoy reading books in groups, and they often check books out to take home and read to their own children, grandchildren, nephews, and nieces. However, we do move on to adult books; we want our students to read for their own pleasure and English improvement, not just to enhance their reading experience with their children.

There are many suggestions for books to use in the ELL and ABE classroom in the chapters that follow. All the children's books are for ages eight and under. Reading levels for other books are included in the text or the appendixes.

Advantages for Family Literacy

Family literacy is an important component of many ABE and ELL programs, and a book club can help promote family literacy.

As adult learners become competent readers in English, they can begin to enjoy fiction, newspapers, magazines, and other reading materials at home, acting as reading role models for their children. It has long been proven that children who see their parents reading are better readers; the value of parents as role models for their children's reading skills cannot be overstated. As parents themselves learn to ask questions, create images, and make connections to what they read, they can assist their children in making these connections, too.

In our class, we introduce parents to good children's literature and model reading-aloud techniques, encouraging parents to read with their pre-school children to interest them early in the wonderful world of books. As an extra benefit, the parents are able to practice their English.

Advanced Students

For more advanced students, particularly those in community college classes, we suggest the instructor investigate using the many high-quality books mentioned on lists for middle school and high school students that are available at local libraries. Award winners—such as recipients of the Newbury Prize (awarded to books of fiction for middle school-aged children), the Pulitzer Prize, and the American Library Association Booklist Awards—are good choices. See Appendix B for book suggestions. Internet sources with good summaries also abound (see Appendix B).

The addition of a book club to our multilevel ELL classes has been an extremely rewarding process. It is a reflection of our philosophy that reading for fun is an important component of a well-rounded English language program. The book club is definitely not a fill-in activity or an answer to, "What can I do on Monday?" Several class periods may be needed to get a book club going, and periodically it may be necessary to reteach certain concepts or strategies. The addition of the comprehension strategies makes our book club much more than a read-and-discuss activity. Our book club explicitly emphasizes the instruction of strategies on *how* to understand what is being read, skills that serve our adult ELL students in many ways outside and beyond our classroom. The book club is the best way of promoting reading for pleasure and authentic conversation among adult ELL students that we have found.

Perhaps the most compelling evidence to us that the book club is valuable to our students comes from them. In a year-end program evaluation, more than half our students mentioned reading for the book club as one of the elements they especially liked about our class. One student said of the book club: "It's good for comprehension for life."

1

Structuring a Book Club

WE had just finished reading aloud a wonderful Big Book, *Turnips for Dinner* by Joy Cowley, to our adult students. (Big Books are simply enlarged versions of a story book. They are standard aids in elementary classrooms and helpful for any beginning readers. They are good for whole-class read-alouds because everyone can see the pictures.) We were incorporating it into a life-skills unit on shopping and a multicultural unit on foods from around the world. Our students

Two students read aloud during the book club.

laughed, listened, and asked clarifying questions while the book was read. We modeled reading aloud with actor-quality emotion so that our students could read to their children with drama.

"OK," we said. "Now we're going to have a discussion about the book. Get into groups of six and talk about it!"

Our students dutifully arranged themselves into groups of six. One student said, "I like this book."

The others agreed. Yes, it was a good book.

"I like the elephant," another offered.

Yes, yes, everybody liked the elephant.

The silence grew thick. "Why did you like the elephant?" we asked, desperate to jump-start the conversation.

"He's cute."

"He's gray."

"He's big."

"Have you ever seen a real elephant?" we asked.

Of course, everybody had seen a real elephant.

That description of our first book club session reveals how it was less than a resounding success. We were not able to persuade our students to develop conversations and real discussions. Why? They did not know what we wanted; few had experience discussing books, especially in English; and we had not developed a method for encouraging meaningful conversation, conversation generated by them rather than by us, the teachers, and questions from a textbook.

However, we were not discouraged. We regrouped, discussed this setback, and realized that our book club needed structure. We realized we wanted the students to be able to discuss the stories in the ways we do and that in order for students to do that, we needed to make sure they were understanding the reading on many levels.

The Comprehension Strategies

What became the structure of our book club came from the understanding and use of some comprehension strategies, which we first encountered in the book *Mosaic of Thought: Teaching Comprehension in a Reader's Workshop* (Keene and Zimmerman 1997). These comprehension strategies encourage students to make connections to the story and, through the use of a set of prompts and questions that accompany each strategy, communicate these connections to the rest of the discussion group.

The comprehension strategies we use include: **Summaries, Text-to-Self, Text-to-World, Text-to-Text, Sensory Images, Predictions and Inferences,** and **Questions and Inferences.**

Summarizing is useful in ensuring that all the students in the group understand what they have just read. Text-to-Self, Text-to-World, and Text-to-Text connections are sometimes overlapping comprehension strategies that encourage students to use personal experiences and what they know (their background knowledge) to relate to the story. Creating Sensory Images allows students to personalize the story and connect images from it to their own memories. Predictions aid the students in making inferences about the story and generate discussion about what would be likely to happen, given previous events and the nature of the story. They help the students read between the lines. Authentic Questions, aided by inferences, propel readers forward in the story and open up new ideas for themselves and other students.

Comprehension Strategy	What It Is	How It Aids Comprehension
Summary	Short recap of important components of the story	• Checks student understanding of story elements • Brings students up-to-date • Teaches question words and formation
Text-to-Self, Text-to-World, Text-to-Text connections	Relating text to personal experiences, cultural and background knowledge, and to other media	• Helps students use their own experiences and feelings, cultures, current events, and other stories to explain the text • Changes students' understanding of each other • Fosters sense of community
Sensory Images	Using the five senses to enrich the story	• Brings the story to life • Makes story more interesting
Predictions and Inferences	Determining what might happen in the story, given our background knowledge, and what has already happened	• Clarifies students' own thinking • Reveals students' reactions to the story • Reveals misunderstandings about the story
Questions and Inferences	Wondering about characters' actions and motivations	• Clarifies the story's theme • Propels students through the story

Eventually, we anticipate that our students will select more than one comprehension strategy for their discussions. The strategies will become primarily internalized tools for comprehension, and the discussion will be centered on questions they have and inferences they make about the ideas in the text. Their thinking will change as they read and discuss the books. They will process a lot of information, synthesize it, and form an opinion.

Format

As a teaching tool to explain the strategy in the beginning or as a wrap-up, we show the students the stick figures that are shown at the start of Chapters 3–8. We talk about and model how the students' reading can trigger personal connections related to experiences and feelings in their lives. We have a stick figure for each strategy, and often refer to them when reteaching or reminding our students about the comprehension strategies (see pages 37, 43, 51, 60, 69, and 76). When we show students the stick figures, we say: "The reader reads the story. The action and emotions in the story make the reader think of something (about himself or herself, in the world, in another book, etc.)."

To introduce the book club, we use a large chart, like Figure 1 on page 14. We review it as each component is taught. Later, when we introduce adult fiction, we provide it as a handout. We revise this format to suit our needs and what works with the particular students we have. This has evolved through the years. For example, we only summarize the selections of the other groups (#7) when we are doing children's books. Also, in our class, the role of the discussion leader is informal and sometimes nonexistent.

Figure 1: Book Club Format*

1. Select one person to SUMMARIZE for the other group(s).
   - ☐ A-Book-in-Hand
   - ☐ Who? What? Where? When? Why? How?

2. Select a DISCUSSION LEADER. (Optional)

3. Pick a COMPREHENSION STRATEGY to guide your discussion.

   Text-to-Self (personal connections, personal opinions)
   Prompts: "This reminds me of my. . . ." "This reminds me of the time I. . . ." "I think. . . ."
   Queries: How was it the same? How was it different? What would you do if . . .?

   Text-to-World (world connections, cultural connections)
   Prompts: "This reminds me of. . . ." "In my country. . . ."
   Queries: How was it the same? How was it different?

   Text-to-Text (connections to other books, articles, movies)
   Prompts: "I read a book (saw a movie, etc.) like this. . . ."
   Queries: How was it the same? How was it different?

   Sensory Images (what you see, hear, smell, etc. in your mind as you read)
   Prompts: "I see (smell, hear, taste). . . ." "I think (character) is. . . ."
   Queries: "What does (character) look like?" "What do you see in this chapter?" "What does it (sound, taste, feel, smell) like?"

   Predictions and Inferences (based on what you know, make a guess)
   Prompts: "I think . . . will happen because. . . ."
   Queries: What do you think will happen to . . .? What do you think will happen next? Why?

   Questions and Inferences (Authentic versus comprehension questions)
   "What does . . . mean?" "What did the author mean by . . .?" "I wonder why. . . ." "I wonder how. . . ." "I wonder about. . . ."

4. Read the selection. (If you read at home, go on to 5.)

5. Discuss the selections and your reactions and connections. Remember to follow up!

6. Record/write in the Book Log.

7. Summarize your selection for the other group(s).

*A sample of the Book Club Format that you can reproduce and distribute is found on page 115.

Time Line

Typically, we use about two hours a week for seven or eight weeks to introduce and model the book club in our multilevel class. Class meets Monday through Friday, from September through May, so we try to alternate the book club so that it occurs on Friday one week and Monday the next. We generally start new strategies on Friday. That way, if students do not finish their discussions, the next book club is not a whole week away. Our time line varies, depending on the abilities of our students and the other activities we are doing in class.

Four Weeks of Book Club					
Monday	Tuesday	Wednesday	Thursday	Friday	Sat/Sun
				BOOK CLUB: Introduce a new strategy	
Monday	Tuesday	Wednesday	Thursday	Friday	Sat/Sun
BOOK CLUB: Finish old discussion or introduce a new strategy					
Monday	Tuesday	Wednesday	Thursday	Friday	Sat/Sun
				BOOK CLUB: Introduce a new strategy	
Monday	Tuesday	Wednesday	Thursday	Friday	Sat/Sun
BOOK CLUB: Finish old discussion or introduce a new strategy					

For programs that do not have the luxury of meeting every day or that run on a shorter schedule, such as eight weeks, we suggest devoting about a week to the book club, doing something every day to get it started. Then, the book club can be held once a week for about an hour and 30 minutes. In these programs, homework might include the next book club reading so that time in class is devoted to the discussion. However, if your students do not read at home, for whatever reason, reading in class is always time very well spent.

We are very flexible with this schedule, allowing our students' comfort with the strategies and our observations of their proficiency to guide us.

Typical Time Line for Introducing the Book Club to a Two-Hour* Multilevel ELL Class	
Week 1: The Summary	Explain the concept using the chart (see p. 14). Read a children's book and summarize it, using A-Book-in-Hand. Model Book Log entry (see p. 27).
Week 2	Groups read and summarize a children's book, using A-Book-in-Your-Hand.
Week 3: Text-to-Self	Model Text-to-Self using children's book. Model Book Log entry. Introduce concept of discussion leader. Students form groups, choose a leader, and make Text-to-Self connections from modeled book.
Week 4: Text-to-World	Model Text-to-World using a children's book or a newspaper clipping. Students form groups, and make Text-to-World connections from modeled text. Students or teachers fill in Book Log.
Week 5: Text-to-Text	Model Text-to-Text using two children's books. Model Book Log entry. Students form groups, read a variety of teacher-selected children's books, and make Text-to-Text connections. Fill in Book Log.
Week 6: Sensory Images	Model Sensory Images using calendars or a passage from a book (no pictures). Students form groups and create sensory images. Fill in Book Log.
Week 7: Predictions and Inferences	Model predictions using children's book. Students form groups, read a variety of children's books, and make predictions. Fill in Book Log.
Week 8: Questions and Inferences	Model authentic questions using children's book. Students form groups, read a variety of children's books, and develop questions. Fill in Book Log.
Week 9: Introduce Adult Fiction	Hand out and review Book Club Format (see p. 14). Students form groups to read and discuss Chapter 1 of Adult fiction. Teacher circulates from group to group.

*Assumes devoting about one and a half hours for the book club since it's unlikely one would be able to devote all two hours of class to the book club.

After the introductory schedule, with stick figure symbols posted as reminders, and using the book club format, continue with each chapter, as shown in Week 9. If students are in different chapters because they read at different paces, group them accordingly. It should take a class using this introduction schedule about ten weeks *after* the eight weeks of modeling to finish *Flor.*

Starting with Children's Books

We use children's books to model the strategies for the class, introducing each one slowly, and explaining and demonstrating it. We select books that are very easy to read and understand and contain pictures that help tell the story so that students are not struggling to grasp the elements of the story, the comprehension strategies, and the book club format at the same time.

Generally, we select a children's book that we think is particularly good for teaching the target strategy (see Chapters 3 through 8 for specific suggestions). We also like to tie the books into the monthly theme or topics we are discussing. For example, we might use *Mama Do You Love Me?*, a book in which an Inuit girl probes the depth of her mother's patience and love, in a month when we are also talking about Native Americans.

Before we read the book to the class, we read it ourselves, using sticky notes to help us remember our own good connections. Then we read the book aloud to the whole class, generally without interruption. As we develop a summary and then talk our way through our connections to the story, we refer to the sticky notes so that our students can see how we remember talking points and ideas.

(See Appendix B for other good books for higher-level classes, academic programs, or ABE students.)

Forming Groups

After reading the children's book and hearing our own reactions to it, the students form groups of five or six and use the strategy to discuss the book. This does not come automatically. We roam the room during this time, sit in on discussions, and push students to participate. If we notice students are reluctant to speak, we ask questions related to the strategy such as, "Did anything like what happened to Elena ever happen to you?" (text-to-self) or "How would a mother in your culture feel if her child wanted to run away?" (text-to-world)

We encourage students to use dictionaries and help each other explain their thoughts. We want them to continue to ask questions and negotiate meanings until the speaker's intended message is clear.

We wrap up these early book club sessions by asking each group to share what they talked about with the other groups.

Developing Independence

The next step is to aid students in developing independence in selecting comprehension strategies. Often, we divide the students according to ability, sometimes with a mix of higher and lower students, sometimes with students of like-ability together, and ask them to select a discussion leader. This person is responsible for keeping track of time and keeping the discussion in English and on the topic. He or she takes over part of the role previously played by the teacher. The discussion leader asks which strategy the students want to think about as they read, and the whole group agrees on the main focus for that session. Keeping early book club discussions to one strategy at a time helps prevent students from getting confused and aids them in really understanding each strategy. However, the discussion leader will usually not stop a conversation because someone is making a text-to-text connection when the group has agreed to make text-to-world connections. An experienced discussion leader might point out the difference, but usually the conversation just keeps flowing, with follow-up discussion about whatever connections the students make. In fact, if many different connections from all the comprehension strategies are being made, it is probably time to stop selecting a single strategy, as the groups are likely on their way to synthesizing.

Having a discussion leader is optional. Sometimes it works and sometimes it doesn't, depending on the personalities and language levels of the participants in the group. If the students can follow the book club format and keep the conversation going in English, discussion leaders aren't necessary. However, if the group gets sidetracked and reverts to native language discussions, then it is useful.

We give each group its own pad of sticky notes, and then students read for 20 to 30 minutes. An alternative to reading in class is to give students the material to take home. Sometimes we introduce the material and have students read some of it (or a chapter, in the case of a longer book) in class. Then, we tell them that their homework for the next book club session is to read the rest of the assignment. We have noticed that this technique seems to motivate students who need a longer time to read and understand each chapter to participate more fully in class.

What are we doing while the students are reading? Reading! Usually, we read one of the books the students are reading. We glance up occasionally to see if anyone needs help, but we want to emphasize the joy and importance of the whole class being engaged in reading (a technique called *sustained silent reading*, or SSR, in elementary, middle, and high schools).

After reading, the group agrees on a one- or two-sentence summary of what they have read. Then, the discussion leader asks the question associated with the comprehension strategy the group has chosen. For example, a Text-to-World question might be: "Is there anything in the story that reminds you of your country?" The leader might also start the discussion with, "In my country. . . ." Then, the discussion leader follows up on the connection, regardless of who made it, and encourages others to comment before sharing other connections. In this way the book club becomes more of a conversation rather than simply a string of comments about the book.

After 20 to 30 minutes of discussion, the students write a few sentences in a Book Log. They may read their entries to the other groups so that all the students can get an idea of what the others were discussing. This is most appropriate when the groups are all reading different stories.

During these initial sessions, we assess through observation and questions whether discussions are flowing smoothly, whether conversations are dying out or being enthusiastically pursued. If the groups seem to be struggling, we try to pinpoint the problems and provide more modeling, either in successive book club sessions or right there, taking over the discussion leader role for a short time.

Once the groups are doing well, we introduce our high-beginning to advanced students to adult fiction in the form of *Flor's Journey to Independence* or one of the other stories we've written. Low-beginning students continue to read children's books until their English improves enough for them to move on to the adult fiction. Our intermediate students usually read the modified versions of our books (two pages per chapter versus ten). Some beginning students want to try reading the modified version of *Flor,* and although we feel it might be too difficult for them, we let them take a chapter or two home to try it.

Using *Flor* and Fiction for Adults

Flor is the first book in a series of fiction written with adult ELL students as the target audience. These are gripping, realistic, and dramatic tales that address genuine issues that newcomers to this country encounter, including preconceived notions or stereotypes they have about the United States. The situations in these books mirror many of the problems our students are facing. The stories are written using vocabulary and phrases that our students can use every day, and they provide important cultural and economic lessons in the context of an interesting story.

Our characters have a community ELL class in common. The protagonists are from different countries and face unique sets of problems. Several of the chapters include a journal entry. As the books progress, these entries show the main character's improving English skills as well as provide updates about what has happened in the interim, between chapters or passage of time within a chapter.

Our students, who range widely in English ability levels and socio-economic and educational backgrounds, love *Flor* and enjoy when we discuss what is happening to her. One Hungarian student, who read the first chapter and said he did not want to finish it because "It's just a soap opera," persevered anyway, and by the middle of the book, was enthusiastically discussing working conditions and labor protections around the world.

You may elect to use other pieces of fiction. If the reading is high-interest, apply the same processes as discussed here for *Flor.*

Alternative Introduction Schedules

As an alternative to the introduction schedule (page 16), we often model a comprehension strategy using a children's book and then have the students use *Flor* and the other similar books to try out the strategy.

Typical Time Line for Introducing Book Club to a Multilevel ELL Class Using *Flor* and Children's Books in a Two-Hour Class	
Week 1: The Summary	Explain the rationale for reading in class. Explain the book club concept using the book club format (p. 14). Read a children's book and summarize it, using the Book-in-Hand. Model Book Log entry.
Week 2: *Flor* summaries Reading: 20–30 minutes Summaries: 30 minutes Book Log: 20 minutes Debrief: 30 minutes	**Students read *Flor,* Ch. 1.** Students form groups and summarize, using the Book-in-Hand. Each group makes a Book Log entry. Debrief as a class.
Week 3: Text-to-Self Modeling: 1 hour Discussion: 30 minutes Book Log: 20 minutes	Model Text-to-Self using children's book. Model Book Log entry. Introduce concept of discussion leader. Students form groups, choose a leader, and make Text-to-Self connections from *Flor,* Ch. 1. Each group makes a Book Log entry.
Week 4: Text-to-World Modeling: 45 minutes Reading: 30 minutes Discussion: 20 minutes Book Log: 15 minutes	Model Text-to-World using a children's book or a newspaper clipping. **Students read *Flor,* Ch. 2,** form groups, and make Text-to-World connections. Each group makes a Book Log entry.
Week 5: Text-to-Text Modeling: 1 hour Reading: 20 minutes Text-to-Text: 20 minutes Book Log: 10 minutes	Model Text-to-Text using two children's books. Model Book Log entry. Students form groups, read a variety of teacher-selected children's books, and make Text-to-Text connections.
Week 6: Sensory Images Modeling: 1 hour Reading: 20 minutes Discussion: 20 minutes Book Log: 10 minutes	Model Sensory Images using pictures. Model Book Log entry. **Students read *Flor,* Ch. 3,** discuss their images, and make a Book Log entry.
Week 7: Predictions and Inferences Modeling: 1 hour Discussion: 30 minutes Book Log: 10 minutes Debrief: 10 minutes	Model Predictions and Inferences using children's book. Students form groups and make predictions based on *Flor,* Ch. 3. Each group makes a Book Log entry.
Week 8: Questions and Inferences Modeling: 1 hour Discussion: 20 minutes Book Log: 10 minutes Debrief: 20 minutes	Model authentic Questions and Inferences using children's book. Students form groups and make authentic questions from *Flor,* Ch.3. Each group makes a Book Log entry. Debrief as a class.

See Appendix D for a time line for a one-hour class that meets three times a week.

If you use a schedule similar to this one, make sure students are clear about which chapter they are discussing in their groups. Some students will have read ahead, but caution them not to ruin the story for the other students. This schedule is also good for slower readers. They can take the book home and finish reading a chapter if they do not finish in class. Following this schedule, most classes would finish *Flor* in about 15 weeks.

A third option would be to have the students read a chapter of *Flor* for you and then model the comprehension strategy you want to teach with the *Flor* chapter. This works well with intermediate students and higher and would also be a good schedule for ABE students. Most classes would finish *Flor* in 10 to 12 weeks using this option.

Reteaching

One morning Barbara walked into a class, and after the morning routine, asked students to get in groups for the book club. A lively Ukrainian student asked, "Hey, what is this book club?"

Barbara looked around the room and realized that, of the 15 students present, only four had been in class since the first day. (We have open enrollment so new students can join the class at any time.) The others were too new to have experienced book club modeling. Thinking on her feet, Barbara explained the concept of the book club and pulled out a chapter of *Flor*. She gave a dramatic reading and then modeled summarizing, with the help of the four long-standing students.

Later, as we debriefed, we realized we were going to have to reteach comprehension strategies to our many new students. The problems were that we also had at least as many long-time students, and we wanted to continue reading adult fiction, rather than going back to the children's literature.

We decided to use summaries of chapters of *Flor* in whole-class discussions about the comprehension strategies. To model, we, as instructors, developed a summary of each chapter with the help of students who had already been in class and had read the first chapters. This made it possible for the new students to understand the basics of the story. Then, we modeled comprehension strategies from the summaries, again with a lot of help from students who had been in the class. This required that we had prepared and had plenty of connections so that we had good modeling ideas before we went into class. The Book Log helped remind students what they had said earlier in the year or term. We continued this until the new students had caught up with the other students. Recent students benefited from veteran students' knowledge of the strategies. Long-time students were then able to move along in discussions and in their reading.

The chapters that follow include in-depth explanations of the comprehension strategies and the book club format. Ideas for possible connections are suggested as well, and some came from our students. We feel these connections are best used when a discussion comes to a standstill or as an occasional prompt because we want the ideas to come from our students. However, they are good guides if you are using other books.

2

The Book-in-Hand: Summaries

SUMMARIZING is a useful and important tool in determining our students' level of understanding of the action of the story. It also helps other students, who might not have grasped the main idea of the chapter, understand and be able to participate in the discussion. If some students have been absent or have not yet read the book or all the chapters up to that point, summarizing brings the whole group together. In addition, it is a good way to teach the question words *who, what, when, where, how,* and *why*.

After much frustration in attempting to describe a summary, versus a retelling or, worse, a re-reading of the entire book or chapter, we borrowed and adapted an idea from a third grade teacher in the school where our program is housed. It's called the Book-in-Hand.

The five fingers of the hand each contain important question words: *who, what, when, where, why.* Feelings and opinions *(how, did you like it?)* are contained in the palm of the hand. We only include the prompt "How" in the illustration of the palm, but while talking we expand to questions like, *How did it make you feel?* This serves as a reminder to students that we only want to know the most important elements of the story in the summary, not all the little details.

Summarizing Using Goodnight Moon

In a workshop we gave about the book club, one teacher asked how we can use the summary questions without teaching them first. She said she thought the question word *who* was very difficult to teach. We answered that, because we have used a children's book, we have pictures of *who*, and all the other summary words as well. We are teaching the question words with the summary. We have never found them to be difficult as long as we pick quality literature with good illustrations.

We have discovered that an excellent children's book to use for summarizing is *Goodnight Moon* by Margaret Wise Brown. When teaching the summary, we help the students develop a whole question to go with the keyword. First, we read the book aloud to the class. Then, we display the book, turning to appropriate pages as we read. For example, in *Goodnight Moon,* the summary questions and answers our class agreed on were:

Figure 2: The Book-in-Hand

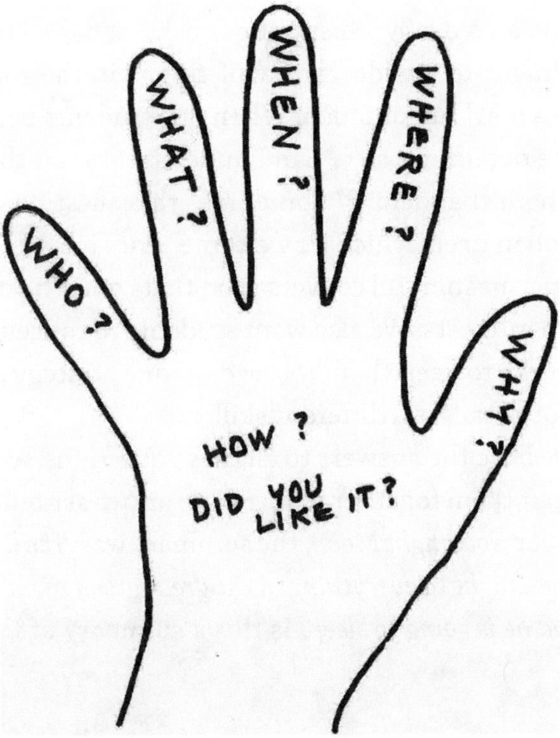

Q: **Who** is the book about?
A: It's about the little bunny.

Q: **What** is he doing?
A: He's saying good night.

Q: **When** does the book take place?
A: The book takes place at night.

Q: **Where** is he?
A: He's in the great green room.

Q: **Why** is he saying good night?
A: He is going to sleep.

We emphasize again that we only want to know the important things in these answers. If you'll remember from *Goodnight Moon,* there is also an old lady whispering "hush," and the little bunny says goodnight to a wide variety of things in the room, from kittens to a bowl full of mush. When our students begin to tell us all these details, we say, "Can I understand what the story is about without that detail?" Sometimes this question generates a discussion in itself, which we welcome, since our ultimate goal is authentic, meaningful conversation that comes from our students' own interests. We also want students to concentrate just on main ideas to keep them focused on one strategy at a time. Reading for details is a different skill.

Once we have the answers to all these questions, we help the students put them together to form one or two sentences about the book. For *Goodnight Moon,* the summary was: *The little bunny is saying goodnight to everything in the great green room because it is night and he is going to sleep.* Is this a summary of this story? Yes.

Summarizing Using Non-Fiction

Often we use books that tie in with the themes we are discussing in class each month. These include excellent non-fiction as well as fiction. We especially like biographies because of the personal connections we can make and the opportunity they offer to enhance the content-based lessons in our class. Non-fiction that has worked especially well in our class includes:

◊ *Frederick Douglass: The Last Day of Slavery* by William Miller, which covers the first part of Frederick Douglass' life, telling how he gained the courage to fight back against slavery. (Intermediate to advanced students, subjects: Civil War, Civil Rights, Black History Month) Reading level grades 3–5

◊ *And Then What Happened, Paul Revere?* by Jean Fritz, which is a classic telling of the ride of Paul Revere. (High-beginning to intermediate students, subjects: Revolution, U.S. History) Reading level grades 4–6

◊ *A Movie in My Pillow* by Jorge Argueta, which is simple but lyrical poetry about the author's Salvadoran childhood and new life in San Francisco. (High-beginning to intermediate students, subjects: Immigration, pride in one's country/heritage) Reading level grades 1–3

Summarizing Chapters

When we start reading adult fiction, we talk about summaries again, but now that we are summarizing every chapter and not a whole book each time we read, we have to decide what the important questions are. We can usually start with, *Who is the chapter about?* or *Who are the characters in the chapter?* We then have to decide if the location is important or whether we already know it, and whether the time of day is relevant. At first, we talk about all these questions, but the students quickly understand that we really only want to know the main events that occurred in each chapter.

Students sometimes focus on different aspects of the chapter than we or fellow students might. We think this is another exciting opportunity for enriching dialogue about the story, especially since early in a story, it may not be perfectly clear to everyone what will become a main event. This is one of the benefits of using fiction.

We record the student's summaries of the adult fiction on chart paper so that anyone who missed class can easily catch up. At the beginning of a book club session, our students take turns reading these chapter summaries out loud.

Summarizing Using *Flor*

Summarizing the first chapter of *Flor* was a good way to reteach how to select important questions. We started by asking all the questions in the Book-in-Hand: who? what? when? where? why? how? did you like it? (as shown on page 27).

Q: **Who** appears in the chapter?
A: Flor, Betina, Maria, Ricardo, the taxi driver, and the landlady.

Q: **Who** are the most important characters?
A: Flor, her daughter Betina, and her husband Ricardo.

We had to talk about this a little. Of course, the beginning of the book can sometimes be misleading in terms of who is ultimately an important character—but that is okay. First, we had to figure out who everyone was. We agreed that Flor was the main character and Betina was her daughter. Ricardo was Flor's husband, and Maria was Ricardo's sister. As we talked, we made a family tree on the board so that relationships were clear to all levels of students. We had recently finished a life skills unit on the family, which included family trees, so this tied in well.

Figure 3: Betina's Family Tree

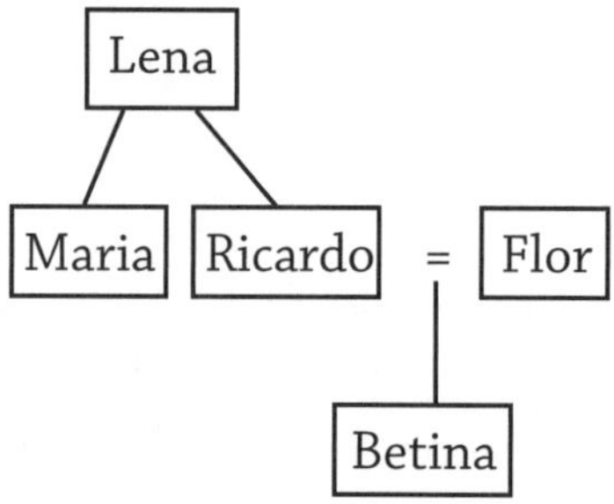

Finally, we decided Maria, the taxi driver, and the landlady were not as important in the summary as the other three characters because it does not seem, based on Chapter 1, that the story was about them. Students are actually using life experiences, inferencing, and text-to-media connections to determine that Ricardo must be important where others are not.

Q: **What** is Flor doing?
A: She and Betina are returning on the bus from a three-month visit to Mexico.

Q: **What** happens when she gets off the bus?
A: No one meets her at the bus. She goes home, and her apartment is empty. There are no clothes and no furniture.

Q: **Where** are they?
A: They are in Denver.

Q: **When** does the story take place?
A: Now.

At this point we stopped again. We asked the students if, having read the first chapter, they thought these last two questions provided important information. We decided they did not because the reader could probably follow the action of this particular story without them. We reiterated that a summary leaves out all the details that make a story interesting to follow page after page, and just lays bare the important facts or basic storyline. As teachers, you may not always agree with what students decide in terms of how important these facts are, but that can prompt good discussion later during the book club.

Q: **Why** is the apartment empty?

A: Ricardo has a new family. He took everything from the apartment and moved in with the new family.

We had answered all the questions contained in the fingers of the hand. We were ready to try writing a summary. We asked the students to think of a couple of sentences that included all the elements of the important questions. After some discussion, they came up with:

> *Flor and Betina found an empty apartment when they came back from Mexico. Ricardo left them to be with his new family.*

We read this aloud. One student asked, *Who is Betina?* The other students replied: *She is the little girl! She is the daughter of Flor and Ricardo.* Another student asked about the empty apartment. *Who did it belong to?* We realized the summary needed a little clarification, so after a discussion of possessive pronouns, we modified it to read:

> *Flor and her daughter, Betina, found their apartment empty when they came back from a trip to Mexico. Flor's husband, Ricardo, left them to be with his new family.*

We save talking about the questions in the palm of the hand *(Did you like it? Why or Why not? How did it make you feel?)* for the group discussions. The palm questions bring in specific opinions that the students need to support; a kind of evaluation, which is a higher-order thinking skill. For example, if a student says she liked the chapter, she must tell why she liked it. Maybe she finds Flor to be brave, or maybe she just finds the situation interesting. If she does think Flor is brave, she needs to say what Flor did to show this.

Troubleshooting

We encounter two problems with summarizing every chapter at the beginning of the book club. The first is that sometimes students will skip chapters in the book, relying on the summary to give them enough information to read the next chapters. We try to be understanding about our students' busy schedules, yet encourage them to read. Occasionally, when several students seem to get bogged down, having missed a few classes or not having time to read outside of class, we will read a chapter aloud to the whole class. Our students enjoy this, and it seems to energize them to keep going. Or, we suggest they read the modified version, just to refresh their memories or clarify thoughts.

The second problem occurs when some students have read much farther in the book and "let the cat out of the bag" about what happens in later chapters. We discourage them from doing this, but if it happens we might summarize the chapters for the slower group and not the advanced group.

As mentioned earlier (see page 23), sometimes comprehension strategies have to be retaught. We often use the summaries the students have developed to do this, modeling our own reaction to an element of a chapter and then asking the whole class key questions to elicit conversation and elucidate the comprehension strategy.

For example, in Chapter 3 of *Flor,* the summary might be: Flor still wonders why Ricardo left her. But Lena agrees to take care of Betina, and Flor finds a pre-school for Betina and an English class for herself. After presenting this summary, Jennifer tells the class about a text-to-self connection: "This reminds me of when I was trying to find daycare for my new baby many years ago. I interviewed 10 or 15 people! Flor is lucky in this one thing. She finds a pre-school right away."

Then, she asks the whole class questions using versions of the prompt questions. Good questions could be, *Has anyone else ever worried about finding daycare? Have you ever left your child with a baby-sitter? Do you think pre-school and daycare are the same?* As students answer, the teacher models follow-up questions and comments, to encourage a conversation. Questions like, *What did you do next?* and *How did you feel when that happened?* and comments like *Tell me more* are good for follow-up.

Pretty quickly, students will be making their own text-to-self connections, moving away from teacher-generated questions.

3

Personal Connections: Text-to-Self

Prompts: This reminds me of the time I. . . .
This reminds me of my. . . .

Queries: How was it the same?
How was it different?
What would you do if. . .?

THE Text-to-Self comprehension strategy helps the student relate the text to his or her own life, including past experiences and background knowledge. It is one of the most useful strategies in helping students understand and make personal connections to the text by associating it with their own feelings about things that happened to them, their families, or their friends. This strategy is one that will serve students well if they pursue academic study. Once students realize that they are supposed to find connections to their own life and experiences, they will never see reading the same way again.

As we discuss Text-to-Self with our students, we tell them that they do not have to reveal any personal details that make them uncomfortable. We realized this was necessary after a whole-class discussion of Flor's decision to live with her brother. She had realized that she could not make it on her own, and she feared that her estranged husband, Ricardo, was going to try to take their daughter, Betina. A visiting teacher shared a Text-to-Self connection about her brother, who had lost his job and had to take his family and live with their parents. Soon, some students were uneasily sharing personal stories. Although we do discourage this, it sometimes happens.

Although some students felt safe and comfortable sharing their painful experiences, some did not. One student told us later that she did not like the Text-to-Self comprehension strategy. We had not made it clear that students could change the direction of Text-to-Self connections simply by making a new association, rather than feeling compelled to tell their own distressing stories. We want our students to feel at ease; this is not a therapy session.

Now, we tell students while we are modeling Text-to-Self connections not to share stories that make them uncomfortable. We are very clear; we might say, "If you have a connection that makes you very sad, you don't have to tell us." To remind them they do not have to share connections that are similar to those that their fellow students might want to tell us, we say, "You can share a happy connection if you think the discussion is getting too personal." Mostly we stress the important thing is that they make a connection, not that they tell anyone about it.

Figure 4: Text-to-Self

Text-to-Self Using *The Little Old Lady Who Was Not Afraid of Anything*

The stick figures, prompts, and questions help students get started and clarify their connections. With the stick figure illustrations we say, *The reader reads the story. The actions and emotions make him or her think about something that happened to him or her and how he or she felt.* As with all strategies, we first model with the whole class, and then form groups to practice the strategy.

To model Text-to-Self, we read *The Little Old Lady Who Was Not Afraid of Anything* by Linda Williams, a book about how a woman's walk in the woods becomes a terrified race to her house with disembodied clothing and a jack-o'-lantern hot on her heels. We asked how the little old lady felt. Students answered that first she was not afraid, but then she became scared. *Have you ever been unafraid in a scary situation?* we asked. Students offered their stories, and we listed them on the board.

Then, we formed small groups to discuss these personal connections. One student focused not on the lack of fear, but on why she should be afraid, before telling her own story. She said of the little old lady, "Oh, she is scared! I would be scared of that head!" She thought for a moment and then said, "Last night I was scared. The wind was blowing very hard. It knocked at my house."

Other students agreed, but one said, "The wind can't knock at your house. A tree was blowing."

Clarification was needed: Had the wind blown a tree limb, which knocked against the student's house, or did something else knock against her house? Maybe her house had been knocked down? Quite a bit of conversation followed, with dictionary pages flying, before the student was able to tell what really happened. The sound of the wind rushing by her house had frightened her. Another student asked why, and the discussion continued with students talking about what things made them afraid.

Text-to-Self Using *The Princess Bride*

The Princess Bride by William Goldman (Reading level grades 9–12) is a very funny fairy tale for adults. It is supposedly written by S. Morgenstern and abridged (only the "good parts" left in) by Goldman. Interwoven with the tale are the author's comments about the book, which both explain and confuse.

In *The Princess Bride,* the most beautiful girl in the world marries the handsomest prince, because she thinks that the farm boy she loves has fallen prey to the Dread Pirate Roberts. The prince turns out to be a scoundrel, and the farm boy turns out to be alive, and after many improbable adventures, the beautiful girl and the farm boy end up happy together . . . sort of. This book is appropriate for advanced students. It has the advantage of having been made into a movie, which could be shown in pieces with the book, or after the whole book is read.

In Chapter 1, we are introduced to the farm boy, Westley; the beautiful girl, Buttercup; a glamorous countess; and her husband, the count. Buttercup realizes that she loves Westley after she sees how the countess looks at him. When she declares her love, he promptly leaves for America to make his fortune and disappears; he is attacked by the Dread Pirate Roberts. At the end of the chapter, sorrow has made Buttercup evolve from merely the eighth most beautiful woman in the world to the most beautiful woman in a hundred years.

Because this book is a comedic farce, a good Text-to-Self question might be: *What would you do if you were the most beautiful man or woman in a hundred years?* This could be a very amusing book club discussion as students imagine what they would do if they were Westley or Buttercup, or if they were the most beautiful man or woman now, in the 21st century.

As the teachers, we would model our answers to the question and then start a whole class discussion of the same Text-to-Self query. Students' ideas of beauty and how it relates to and has affected their lives might enter the conversation. Then, we would put students into groups to discuss their own Text-to-Self connections to the chapter. Another question might be: *Have you ever spent time away from someone you loved? How did you feel?*

Other topics that could be discussed include fairy tales, stereotypes, the role of women in various cultures, class stratifications, and heroism.

Text-to-Self Using Other Children's Books

◊ *The Runaway Bunny* by Margaret Wise Brown
A little bunny tells his mother he's going to change form and run away from home. She follows him on his imagi-

nary journey, changing into complementary, protective characters. He realizes that, no matter what, she loves him.
Text-to-Self connections: Parental love, parenting skills, one's childhood, youthful fantasies

◊ *Suppertime for Frieda Fuzzypaws* by Cyndy Szekeres*
When Frieda sees the cookies her daddy made, she decides they are going to be all she has for dinner. Her parents have a different idea.
Text-to-Self connections: healthy eating habits, setting limits

Text-to-Self Using *Flor*

In the Chapter 2 of *Flor*, Flor applies for a job at Burger King®. She is nervous because she does not speak English and has never worked before. She fills out an application and has a conversation with the Burger King manager, who hires her on the spot. For a whole-class discussion, we made connections to our own first job experiences. Jennifer's first job, for example, was selling pots and pans door-to-door in rural New Jersey. She hated it, and she quit after the first day. But Flor can't quit, even if she does not like the job. She has to support Betina.

After sharing this connection, we asked students about their first jobs. Did anyone ever have a job in a fast-food restaurant? How was it like Flor's job? How was it different? Even beginning students can say a few words about where they work, like "My job is not the same. I work at night." Other students generally ask for more details, and a conversation starts.

We usually close the whole-class discussions with a reminder about the kind of connections we have been making.

*Note: The book by Cyndy Szekeres is out of print, but at the time of this book's publication, it was available on *Amazon.com*.

4

Cultural Connections: Text-to-World

Prompts: This reminds me of. . . .
In my country (town, city, culture). . . .

Questions: How was it the same?
How was it different?

TEXT-to-World connections are made when we relate the text we are reading to the world at large. Current events, societal concerns, and cross-cultural issues are all appropriate Text-to-

World subjects. This strategy helps students understand the text by relating it to their culture or to events happening in the world today. Discussions can change students' understanding of the book and of each other. Talking about our cultures fosters acceptance and a sense of community in class.

Text-to-World discussions can be particularly fascinating in the multicultural ELL classroom where the students are usually eager to know about each other's countries. Cultural differences between ABE students from different parts of the country and with diverse interests or socio-economic levels could be equally good discussion generators. We bring what we know about the world-at-large to these conversations; we are sharing information.

Connecting the text to a breaking news story can provide opportunities for students to hear a variety of opinions and sometimes hear about something they missed or didn't understand because of their English level.

Text-to-World Using a Newspaper Article

Newspaper articles can be wonderful media for modeling Text-to-World connections. Several years ago, during elections in November, we found an article in the *Denver Post* entitled "Mail Voting Puts Stamp on Election." It was about Denver's trial run for the general public with voting by mail.

We first rewrote the article using English simpler than the original. We gave students both the rewritten and original versions and then read the rewritten version aloud. After summarizing, we asked, "Can you vote by mail in your country?" No one said yes. In fact, it turns out that they were not very interested in that question, but one student raised a question about something else in the article. He said, "What does this mean, 'Elections for the president or governor are held in even-numbered years like 2000 or 2002.' Do you vote for president every two years?"

Figure 5: Text-to-World

Someone else said she thought all elected officials had four-year terms. Another said, no, six-year terms like the presidential term of office in Mexico. Along with a discussion of the sentence from the article, we began to talk about term limits and election practices in Mexico and Argentina as well as that in the United States (since this is an important question for citizenship exams).

Text-to-World Using *Flor*

A hot topic in our classroom was whether Ricardo was justified in leaving Flor (Chapter 1). Some students thought three months was a long time to go away and that Ricardo could not be expected to wait for her, even if they did have a child. Others felt different. A Turkish woman said, "In my country, a woman would not leave a man for so long." Since Ricardo and Flor are originally from Mexico, this led to a discussion of what was culturally acceptable for women in Mexico versus Turkey and the other countries represented in the class. Although this was a whole-class discussion we, as teachers, did not participate much. Instead, we acted as facilitators, helping students understand each other when necessary. We sometimes will offer an opinion of how an American might react to the situations Flor is in. Our students enjoy this, but we only do it occasionally, as this participation by us can become a lecture on U.S. customs. The class finally wrapped up this discussion by bringing in a current event: the position of women in Afghanistan under the Taliban.

Text-to-World naturally lends itself to comparison/contrast discussions. If ideas are mapped out on the board, they can be easily put into a comparison/contrast format and written up in a composition. For example, in *Flor* (Chapter 2), Betina's grandmother makes her tortillas and hot chocolate for breakfast. A comparison/contrast chart with contributions from our multicultural students might look like this:

Breakfast around the World				
USA	Mexico	Morocco	Indonesia	Belgium
Cereal, toast, orange juice, coffee, eggs	Tortillas, hot chocolate	Bread, apricot jam, café-au-lait	Soup made with rice	Cheese, meat, bread

Text-to-World Using *Charlotte's Web*

The classic *Charlotte's Web* by E. B. White (Reading level grades 4–6) is a beautiful story of the unlikely friendship between a pig and a spider. Wilbur is raised by hand and grows from the runt of the litter to a fine pig. While growing, he meets Charlotte, the beautiful and clever spider living in the doorway of the barn.

Eventually, Charlotte devises a plan to save Wilbur from his fated conversion to bacon and ham. In Chapter 11, Charlotte's plan to save Wilbur takes shape: She writes the words "SOME PIG!" in her web. When the farmer sees the words, he visits his minister to try to make sense of the miracle.

Although written for older children, *Charlotte's Web* is appropriate for advanced adults because of the writing style and the message that miracles are all around us. An interesting Text-to-World discussion might arise from asking how miracles are viewed in the countries represented in the class. A teacher from the United States might start with, "In my country, we are skeptical of miracles. Even though *Charlotte's Web* is an American classic, I don't think most Americans would believe that miracles can actually happen." The discussion could run the gamut from scientific explanations of "miracles" to why Americans love tabloid newspapers with sightings of Elvis and births of 200-pound babies.

Other topics that might be explored are the nature of friendship, farm life, how animals are viewed, and county fairs.

Text-to-World Using Other Children's Books

◊ *Rudolph the Red-Nosed Reindeer* by Anonymous
Rudolph, a funny-looking reindeer with a red nose, saves a foggy Christmas from disaster by guiding Santa's sleigh through the gloom.
Text-to-World connections: holiday traditions

◊ *Too Many Tamales* by Gary Soto
A little girl slides her mother's ring onto her finger and then helps make tamales for Christmas. The ring disappears, and she and her cousins frantically eat all the tamales in an attempt to find it. They are unsuccessful, but when she goes to confess her crime, she looks down at her mother's hand. There is the ring!

Text-to-World connections: cultural reactions, holiday foods, holiday traditions, parenting, male vs. female roles in family

Troubleshooting

Occasionally, after reading a chapter, our students do not want to discuss using the one comprehension strategy they have chosen. We allow them to switch because spontaneity is much more important than making students stick to their chosen strategy. After all, the aim is lively talking in our tension-free learning environment.

One group chose Text-to-World for a chapter of *Flor* in which Flor finds her husband, only to have him tell her he has no intention of giving her money to help her with food, rent, or child care. One student, upon finishing the chapter, immediately made a prediction: "I am afraid Flor will not be able to take care of her child. Her husband is going to take her away."

This prediction sparked a debate about whether he should have the child, whether it was Flor's fault that her husband left her, and finally, in a more Text-to-World context, if it would be acceptable in the various cultures represented among the students for the man to take the child instead of the woman.

When making Text-to-World connections, we steer away from judgmental debates about cultural differences. Those discussions are not intended to determine that any one way is better than any other. We do not want to alienate each other and further perpetuate stereotypes. Rather, as an ultimate goal, with these frank and open conversations, we strive for peace and understanding by putting faces and names on strangers.

In one book club discussion, a student asked, "Which country has the most beautiful women in the world?" She quickly answered herself: "I think Korea." Naturally, she was Korean.

The other students in the group laughed, a little awkwardly, and a student who had been in book club for two years used her knowledge of successful book club discussions to respond: "In your country, what is considered beautiful?" This took the discussion to a different, more relaxed place for all the students in the group. As the teacher, you can always use the prompts to bring a potentially tense conversation to a more comfortable position for everyone.

A book club student focuses her reading to make the necessary text connections.

5

Media Connections: Text-to-Text/Media

Prompts: I read a book (saw a TV show, etc.) like this.
This reminds me of a book I am reading.
(Character X) is like (Character Y) in a book I read.

Queries: How is it the same?
How is it different?

TEXT-to-Text connections are made when we compare the book we are reading with some other book, poem, article, radio program, television show, or movie we have seen. The connections can be as simple as noting that the illustrators of two children's books are the same or as complex as talking about how the motivations of characters in two different books are similar but the consequent actions are different, and why. As with Text-to-Self and Text-to-World connections, Text-to-Text connections help our students activate prior knowledge to aid in understanding the book they are discussing.

We include movies and television shows in the Text-to-Text comprehension strategy because many of our students are more likely to watch them than they are to read a book. Also, as our student pointed out, *Flor* is like a soap opera, and a number of our students are hooked on *novelas,* the Spanish-language soaps on television and the radio. Interesting connections can follow when a student comments that she thinks Flor is acting like a certain character she enjoys from her favorite *novela*.

Text-to-Text Using *Whose Mouse Are You?* and *Where Are You Going, Little Mouse?*

Text-to-Text connections using children's books can take many forms. We can connect illustrations, authors, different versions of the same story, series with a running character, and themes. The books *Whose Mouse Are You?* and *Where Are You Going, Little Mouse?* by Robert Kraus are particularly good, because students can make Text-to-Text connections on a number of levels.

First, we read both books. Then, using some of the prompt words, we said, "*Where Are You Going Little Mouse?* reminds me

Figure 6: Text-to-Text

of the first book we read, *Whose Mouse Are You?* What is the same about these books?" We wrote the answers on a piece of chart paper under the heading: Things that Are the Same. Then we asked for things that are different and recorded them as well.

Things that Are the Same	Things that Are Different
The author: Robert Kraus	*The action:* Little Mouse goes looking for a new family but realizes his real family loves him.
The illustrator: Jose Aruego	*The action:* Little Mouse feels abandoned by his family until he realizes he can bring them all together again.
The main character: Little Mouse	
The theme: The stories are both about family love.	

As an alternative, these children's books, or other books with good Text-to-Text connections, can be used in earlier lessons to model other comprehension strategies. Then, during a lesson modeling Text-to-Text, the students will already have been exposed to works that lend themselves to this comprehension strategy.

Sometimes, for variety, and once our students really have this comprehension strategy under their belts, we compare two very different books, such as *The Very Hungry Caterpillar* by Eric Carle and *Goodnight Moon*. The students have to push themselves to come up with items of comparison, but it can be fun and not so academic or serious. The chart shows a different graphic organizer using these two very different books.

Items of Comparison	Goodnight Moon	The Very Hungry Caterpillar
Author	Margaret Wise Brown	Eric Carle
Main characters	Bunny and Little Old Lady	The caterpillar
Setting	The great green room	The whole world
Theme	The comfort and reassurance of a going-to-bed ritual.	The metamorphosis of a caterpillar into a butterfly; being true to one's nature.

Using these items of comparison also allows the instructor to bring in the ideas of setting and theme. Although we have been talking about them in the book club, we haven't mentioned them explicitly. ABE students and ELL students in college classes can especially benefit from this discussion because more academic courses require recognition of these terms. Also, this kind of graphic organizer could easily lend itself to a writing assignment.

Text-to-Text Using Other Children's Books

- ◊ *Pumpkin Pumpkin* by Jeanne Titherington
  Jamie plants a pumpkin seed in the spring and observes it, step by step, until it becomes an enormous pumpkin in the fall.
- ◊ *The Carrot Seed* by Ruth Krauss
  A little boy plants a carrot seed. Everyone in his family repeatedly tells him it won't grow, but he waters it faithfully. Finally, the seed produces a wheel-barrow-sized carrot.
  Text-to-Text connections: planting vegetables, spring, perseverance
- ◊ *Peanut Butter and Jelly* (any version)
  In this popular play rhyme, a peanut butter-and-jelly sandwich is made and eaten to a rhythmic beat.
- ◊ *This Is the Plate* by Alan Trussell-Cullen
  Another rhyme in which children make a sandwich.
  Text-to-Text connections: Food, lunches, peanut butter-and-jelly sandwiches, rhythmic language, children's songs

We also use different versions of fairy tales and fables, both in book and movie form, for Text-to-Text connections. For example, it can be fun to use a traditional version of *The Three Little Pigs* and compare it to a book like *The True Story of the Three Little Pigs* by John Scieszka, which is told by the wolf. In it, the wolf comes out as misunderstood and maligned, a wolf with a cold who couldn't help his enormous sneezes. Items of comparison can include the pig's characters in each book, the wolf's character, illustrations (traditional versus wacky), how the wolf blew the houses down, and so on.

Also interesting, and a lot of fun, are A. J. Jacobs's *Fractured Fairy Tales*. These are the fairy tales that were featured on the "Rocky and Bullwinkle" show in the late 1950s and early 1960s. Tapes of these shows can be found at some libraries, but the book has 25 of these twisted tales that could be compared with traditional versions. Twelve of the stories are available free at *brownielocks.com/fracturedfairytales.html.*

Text-to-Text with *Man o' War* and *Seabiscuit*

Man o' War (Reading level grades 9–12) is the fictional biography of the great racehorse of the same name, who won 20 of his 21 racing starts. The story is told through the eyes of a fictional stable boy, Danny Ryan. The author, Walter Farley, also wrote the popular children's series, *The Black Stallion.* Man o' War was the grandfather of the famous Seabiscuit, so a good Text-to-Text comparison might be the excellent non-fiction book *Seabiscuit: An American Legend* (Reading level Adult) by Laura Hillenbrand. Although Seabiscuit did not cut the imposing physical figure Man o' War did, he seemed to have the same competitive spirit that made both horses beloved winners.

Because the styles of these books are very different, one way to model Text-to-Text would be for the teacher to summarize the main events of each story, then create a table with items of comparison. Some items of comparison could be the races run and won; the personalities of the horses; the personalities of their owners and trainers; and how the horses were raised, treated, and revered by fans.

Then, if one group reads *Man o' War* and one group reads *Sea Biscuit,* Text-to-Text comparisons might be made between the two groups, rather than within the group on an individual basis. After a brief summary of each story so far, students could develop and talk about how the books—and horses—differ and are the same. In addition, Man o' War raced in the early 1920s and Seabiscuit in the late 1930s, so in future classes, as the books are read, comparisons can also be made of American life in these very different times.

An excellent movie of Seabiscuit's story was made in 2003. If the whole class first reads *Man o' War,* a second Text-to-Text alternative might be to watch the movie *Seabiscuit* and make Text-to-Text comparisons in groups with the two forms of media.

Text-to-Text Using *Flor*

We find comparing soap operas or television dramas to *Flor* works well. We suggest taping an episode of an English-language soap opera, making sure the tape includes the closed-captioning that cable provides, and showing it to students. Students can then get into discussion groups and, using prompts and queries from the discussion leader, make Text-to-Text connections with *Flor*.

In Chapter 7, Flor's daughter, Betina, is injured while being cared for by Flor's good friend, Carmen. Flor rushes to the hospital and stays the night by their unconscious daughter's bed. Ricardo does too. They fight, and, as accusations fly, Betina wakes up. We think a good soap opera to watch after reading this chapter would be an episode of *General Hospital*, especially one in which a medical emergency occurs (although any of the televised soap operas often have medical emergencies). (Because soap operas often repeat conversations and stories over several consecutive days, they are better than medical dramas that are shown in prime-time.)

Krashen (2003) shows that series, where ELL students can follow characters throughout a story or from book to book, are especially compelling to students. Keene and Zimmerman (1997) have indicated that weaker readers benefit from following a character and a plot as they develop. Comparing two books in a series is a good way to model Text-to-Text connections.

Here we provide an example from two of our stories:

Items of Comparison	*Flor's Journey . . .*	*Senem's Hope . . .*
Authors	Barbara Vaille and Jennifer QuinnWilliams	Same
Main characters	Flor, Betina, Ricardo	Senem, Tarkan, Hasan
Setting	Denver	Same
Action	Flor's husband leaves her, and she must provide for herself and her child.	Senem struggles to decide whether she will have a second child in this lonely, dangerous new country.
Theme	A young woman learns to depend on herself.	A woman learns that you can make a family wherever you go.

You could also compare Flor to any work of popular fiction that your students are familiar with, like *The Witch of Blackbird Pond* by Elizabeth George Speare, which more advanced students might know. Here is what the entries might look like.

Items of Comparison	*The Witch of Blackbird Pond*
Author	Elizabeth George Speare
Main Characters	Kit Tyler, the Witch of Blackbird Pond, Nat
Setting	Connecticut Colony, 1687
Action	Free Spirit Kit Tyler struggles to fit into Puritan Connecticut Colony.
Theme	Kit finds inner strength through her hardships and friendship with an outcast and an outsider.

Troubleshooting

We find Text-to-Text to be easy to teach but difficult for our students to practice when engaged in the book club. Text-to-Text does not come as naturally as the other comprehension strategies do. Most of our students watch television (although not necessarily in English), but fewer read newspapers, magazines, or books. We handle this by periodically modeling a new Text-to-Text connection to *Flor* using a newspaper article, movie we have just seen, or book we are reading. However, it would be important to stress Text-to-Text connections with students who want to pursue more academic coursework.

6

The Five Senses: Sensory Images

Prompts: I see (smell, hear, taste, feel). . . .
I can taste the. . . .
I think (character, scene) looks like. . . .

Queries: "What does (character, scene) look like?"
"What do you see in this chapter?"
"What does it (look, sound, taste, feel, smell) like?"
"What is the movie in your mind?"

BARBARA Kingsolver was asked once what she would think about having a movie made of one of her books. She responded that the beauty of a book is that there are as many movies of that particular story as there are people who read it. That is how we first explain Sensory Images to our students—as multi-sensory movies in their minds.

Using sensory images to comprehend a story makes it come alive in the minds of many students. It makes the text more interesting, helps them imagine themselves in the story, and improves enjoyment of the text. For less proficient students, talking about sensory images provides comprehensible input about the words used to describe the five senses of seeing, hearing, smelling, touching, and tasting.

Figure 7: Sensory Images

In *Too Many Tamales* the father leans into the steam rising from the pot of tamales on the stove. The picture in the book provides a rich visual image. But what does he smell? Maybe he smells the rich, earthy aroma of the corn husks and the masa, combined with a hint of the spicy pork filling. When the steam hits his face, what does it feel like? What sound does the boiling water in the pot make, and is the father humming in delight? Can we hear his stomach rumbling in anticipation? These are sensory images.

Perhaps as we read this story, the sensory images evoked remind us of our own experiences with a special food. The first time Jennifer tasted tamales, for example, was in a restaurant in California. She didn't know what to expect, and the tamales looked less than appealing, wrapped in a crackling, rough corn husk. But, the first bite changed her mind; the tamale was moist with a hint of sweetness, which was perfectly complimented by the piquant filling. The tamales in the book probably taste just like that. Because Jennifer can taste those tamales, she identifies more with the whole story, as the children eat all of the Christmas tamales to find a lost ring.

We usually introduce Sensory Images in two steps, first with a calendar picture and then with a book. We use calendar pictures (of which we have collected dozens over the years) to evoke the language needed to describe an image using the senses. UNICEF or Peace Corps calendars are very good for images from around the world. We show the class a picture and tell what we see, hear, smell, taste, and feel. We tell them about our connections to these senses and which experiences in our lives have prepared us to react to the picture in this way.

Then, we show them a second picture and ask what they see. They will usually describe the picture, making some inferences about the action or the characters. Then, we ask them, *What do you think the person in the picture smells? How do you think her dress feels? Is she hot or cold? What are the sounds she hears? What does she taste, hear, feel?*

Meeting outside can be a great way to tap into sensory images during the book club.

Just as we did while modeling, our students make personal connections and inferences along with getting sensory images as they become involved in this exercise. Upon seeing an image of an African village with a tethered goat, one Japanese woman who grew up on a farm told the class, "I smell dung, and I taste goat milk on rice, like when I child." She closed her eyes, licked her lips, and smiled. "Delicious!"

After everyone has a chance to share their sensory images, we either progress to a children's book, reading it to the class without showing the pictures, or straight to adult fiction in groups. It depends on the size of the class and the levels of the various students attending that day.

Sensory Images Using *Ibrahim*

Ibrahim, by Francesc d'A Sales, is the story of a Moroccan boy who loves his life as the son of a market stallkeeper until his friend comes by to tell him that he is going to run away to the desert. Suddenly, Ibrahim wonders if this life in the chaotic Marrakech market will satisfy him. Would he prefer the solitude of the desert? The story abounds with possibilities for Sensory Images.

We start by reading about half of the story. We do not show the pictures, though we stop often to check for understanding, especially if we have many lower-level students in the class. Then, we close the book.

Do you have a movie going in your mind? What do you think Ibrahim looks like? How does the market sound? Is it noisy? What sounds do you hear? We continue until we have a detailed sensory picture of the market and the story characters. Then, we show the pictures. Students' images may be close to those of the illustrator, or completely different. We tell them it does not matter. The story came alive in their minds, helping them understand it in a way that meant the most to them.

Sensory Images Using Other Children's Books

◊ *Where the Forest Meets the Sea* by Jeannie Baker
An Australian boy and his father take a boat trip to a hundred-million-year-old tropical rain forest in North Queensland. The boy plays in the forest, imagining all the animals, aborigines, and events that have come before. This story is particularly good for evoking sounds and smells. The pictures are colorful, detailed collages, making the book good for beginners. The theme is conservation.

◊ *Why Mosquitos Buzz in People's Ears* by Verna Aardema
The animals in the forest are in an uproar because, upon the death of her owlet, Mother Owl has stopped hooting the sun awake. In eternal night, they look for the answer to this tragedy. Once the animals get to the bottom of the

mystery, Mosquito is disgraced and Mother Owl awakens the sun. The language involves lots of noise and movement through the forest. (The book may also result in a discussion of the repercussions of lies.)

Sensory Images Using *A Wrinkle in Time*

In the classic science fiction book by Madeleine L'Engle, *A Wrinkle in Time* (Reading level grades 4–6), a group of gifted children search for the father of two of them on different planets and in different dimensions. Only when one of them, the hot-headed, angry Meg Murry, understands that love is the one force that can outwit evil, are the children successful in returning with Mr. Murry to earth.

The descriptive language in this book is wonderful and, because the children travel to so many different planets, the possibilities for sensory images connections abound. For example, in Chapter 4, Meg and her companions move through time and space using a "tesseract." L'Engle writes of Meg: "She was alone in a fragment of nothingness." A good way to model Sensory Images with this might be to ask students what they think nothingness feels, tastes, sounds, looks, and smells like. Sensory images could be combined with Text-to-Self in this case with the question, *Have you ever experienced anything close to nothingness? Which senses were you missing?*

As the chapter continues, Meg's senses return to her, allowing for a discussion of what the students see, etc. *A Wrinkle in Time* requires imagination and a little patience to read because it is a mystery as well as a science fiction adventure.

Other themes that can be explored in this book are the power of love, the nature of faith, the source of evil, and whether humans are alone in the universe. *A Wrinkle in Time* is the first book in a trilogy. The other two, which follow the same characters as they have more adventures, grow up, and get married, are *A Wind in the Door* and *A Swiftly Tilting Planet*.

Sensory Images Using *Flor*

As Flor and Ricardo sit beside Betina's hospital bed, students must draw on their background knowledge to make Sensory Images. Perhaps the hospital smells like stale food, cleaning supplies, and some kind of medicine—exactly what we don't know. Some students might like this smell, especially if, like a few of ours, they work in a hospital. Others might find it frightening or impersonal.

Betina is hooked up to a monitor, which probably beeps now and then. We might hear the rustle of clothing and bodies stirring as Ricardo and Flor try to get comfortable. Occasionally, we might hear the quiet sound of their discussion. It is probably cold or overheated in the room, as hospitals always seem to be one or the other, and the chairs feel soft at first but become harder and harder as the night wears on. As the movie is playing in the students' heads, Flor, made courageous by her daughter's accident, finally has the nerve to ask Ricardo to help her financially.

Students' images for the same passage can be very different, depending on their backgrounds and English levels. Sometimes, talking about these differences clarifies the story and highlights areas where one student does not really understand the text. In our class, students have used evidence from the book to help other students change their thinking, a rewarding discussion for all involved.

There are possibilities for Sensory Images in every chapter, and we find students enjoy making them. For beginners, talking about Sensory Images that come from stories is a good way to cover the five senses in a communicative, meaningful way. For more advanced students, making and discussing Sensory

Images help them use descriptive language and synthesize their complete reactions to and feelings about a story. In all cases, Sensory Images are important in making the story come alive for the students and allowing them to use their own images to discuss and understand the story.

Troubleshooting

If the class is intermediate to advanced, Sensory Images can be introduced with descriptive paragraphs from newspapers or magazines, or with descriptive language you have heard. On the occasion of a rare eclipse of the moon by the earth's shadow, we heard the following description on the radio: "The earth's shadow will completely eclipse the moon. The earth will gobble up the moon, bite by bite. Sunsets all over the world will leak their light onto the moon."

This was such an evocative image, and tied in so well with a current event, that we presented it to our students as an introduction to Sensory Images. We had fun drawing a picture of what students thought this looked like. However, it is really a visual image. It is only part of what makes an excellent Sensory Image. In introducing Sensory Images, it is important that the material is broad enough to provide opportunities to explore all the senses.

If beginners are having trouble understanding the idea from pictures only, realia can be used to reinforce the stories. A book like *Peanut Butter and Jelly* (see Chapter 5) might be used, and students could make peanut butter-and-jelly sandwiches. Or, *The Little Old Lady Who Was Not Afraid of Anything* (see Chapter 3) might be read, with a pair of old jeans, a shirt, gloves, a pumpkin, etc. As the story progresses, the students can see, hear, feel, taste, and smell the same things the characters do.

7

What's Next: Predictions and Inferences

Prompt: I think . . . will happen ***because***

Queries: What do you think will happen next?
What do you think will happen to . . . ?
What makes you say that?
Why do you think that might happen?

PREDICTIONS are informed guesses about things students have learned in the story, see in the cover illustrations, or read in the summary on the back of the book. In *Goodnight Moon*, it is unlikely that the little old lady whispering hush is going to suddenly break into an entertaining jitterbug. That wouldn't be consistent with the story. Predictions help our students clarify their thoughts about the story and reveal how they are thinking and reacting to the narrative.

Prediction techniques can be simple, such as reading to a certain page and asking, *What do you think is going to happen next?* The answers may be easy because the text offers obvious clues, as do most children's books. Or, predictions can come from a more subtle, complex analysis of the text; they can come from inferring, or reading between the lines. However, there is a difference between inferring and predictions. In inferring, the reader may never know the answer to the inference. The answers to predictions are known by the end of the story. The prediction either comes true or it does not. We infer ideas. We predict outcomes. Discussion happens when, after a student makes a prediction, we ask the question: *Why do you say that?* The student must provide evidence for the answer, often using an inference. In making a prediction about Flor, one of our students said she thought Flor would get sick because she works so hard. Flor does work hard, but nowhere does the book explicitly state this. In fact, Flor never complains. This was an excellent inference.

For our adult ELL students, the predictions and inferences they make are often biased by their cultures. We find it very interesting to ask why students make the predictions they do; valuable cultural information about the United States and other nations can be shared while students negotiate meaning and learn English.

One simple way to introduce inferences, even before you read, is to act out emotions with your class, and then ask how

Figure 8: Predictions and Inferences

they could tell which emotion you were projecting. (This idea is from *Strategies that Work* [Harvey and Goudvis 2000].) You could make an angry face and ask your students how you are feeling. When they answer, "Angry" (assuming you are a fairly good actor), ask them why. They might have noticed that your eyebrows were furrowed, your eyes looked mad, or your mouth was downturned. Although you never said you were angry, they infer it from your attitude.

Predictions Using *The Very Hungry Caterpillar*

In *The Very Hungry Caterpillar* by Eric Carle, a hungry caterpillar is hatched out of a tiny egg. He eats his way through the days of the week. The language is repetitious: "On Monday, he ate his way through one apple. But he was still hungry. On Tuesday he ate his way through two pears, but he was still hungry." When we finish with Friday, we close the book.

"What do you think will happen next?" we ask.

The students know the pattern. They also may realize the caterpillar has eaten nothing but fruit. Most know caterpillars turn into butterflies. The answers come fast and furious: "I think he's gonna eat six pieces of fruit." "He will make himself a little bed to sleep for becoming a butterfly." "He's getting tired of eating." Someone inevitably suggests he might get fat, or squashed. And someone else always says, "I don't know!" To those students we say, "Guess!"

We list the students' predictions on the board, talk about why they made them, and then continue with the story. On Saturday, the hungry caterpillar eats all sorts of junk and gets a stomachache. On Sunday, he eats one green leaf and makes himself a cocoon. Two weeks later, he emerges as a beautiful butterfly. Eric Carle's colorful butterfly illustration always brings sighs of approval from our students.

Then we go back to the Predictions. If they were true, we mark them with a plus sign, if false, a minus sign (a technique we also borrowed from *Strategies that Work*). If they were inferences, we mark them with an "I" as the chart indicates.

The hungry caterpillar will . . .	**because...**	**True (+), False (–), Inferred (I)**
eat six pieces of fruit . . .	he eats fruit every day.	–
make himself a bed and become a butterfly . . .	that's why he's eating so much, and that's what caterpillars do.	+
get tired of eating . . .	he's exhausted.	I
get fat . . .	he's a pig!	+
get squashed . . .	he ate so much he can't move.	–

Predictions Using Other Children's Books

◊ *Bringing the Rain to Kapiti Plain* by Verna Aardema
Told with the rhythm of "The House that Jack Built," this is the story of how Ki-pat helped end a drought on the Kapiti Plain in Africa by shooting a huge, black rain cloud with an arrow.
Predictions: How do you think the feather dropped by the eagle is going to change the weather? Why do you think that? What do you think Kia-pat will do with the arrow he made?

◊ *Sylvester and the Magic Pebble* by William Steig
Sylvester the donkey finds a magic pebble that allows him to wish for whatever he wants. As he is running home to tell his parents of his wonderful discovery, he encounters a hungry lion. He wishes he were a rock and becomes one, with the magic pebble lying beside him.
Predictions: What do you think will happen to Sylvester? Will Sylvester ever become a donkey again? Why do you think that?

◊ *Fox* by Margaret Wild
Magpie's wing is injured in a fire, and Dog rescues her and gives her a reason to live. But, enraged, envious, lonely Fox can't stand their beautiful friendship.
Predictions: I think Dog and Magpie will become friends. Will Fox eat Magpie? Will the three become friends? (Other themes are loyalty and kindness.)

Predictions and Inferences using *Ella Enchanted*

Ella Enchanted (Reading level grades 4–6) by Ella Carson Levine is a different take on the Cinderella story. Ella is given the "gift" of total obedience as a baby, which makes a lot of trouble for her as she grows up and is put in the charge of her evil stepmother and sisters. The nice thing about this retelling of the old fairy tale is that Ella solves her own problems, breaks the curse through force of will, and emerges triumphant in the end. The book is also amusing because Ella must follow even the silliest, unintended orders.

Making Predictions with this book is a lot of fun because while many students will probably be familiar with the story, the author has changed it enough that knowledge of the original might get the predictor in a little trouble. A good way to model predictions might be to tell the class this is a version of Cinderella with a feminist twist, and then have them speculate what that might mean.

The teacher could make a list of what changes might be required for the story's heroine to act in a less traditional way. For example, the class might speculate that Ella would refuse to take her predicament with the meek goodwill of the traditional Cinderella or she might want to save herself rather than wait to be saved by a prince. Then, have the whole class read Chapter 1 to see how their background knowledge of what feminism means and their familiarity with the story helped them with their predictions.

Ella Enchanted was made into a movie in 2004. Other themes include freedom and self-discovery.

Predictions Using *Flor*

As we read *Flor* our students make constant Predictions and Inferences. "Flor and Ricardo will get back together." "Ricardo is going to try to steal Betina." "Ricardo will try to come back, and Flor will say, 'No.'" "Flor will go to a lawyer, and Ricardo will have to pay child support."

We try to write them all down on chart paper, as in the chart on page 70; as they are answered, we code them with a plus, minus, or an "I." Before the last chapter, we review these predictions. This review has several functions. It is a good excuse to congratulate our students on having read a whole book in English, it reminds them of the details of the story, and it prompts a discussion as to why things turned out as they did. Also, we can see which predictions were correct.

In one class, this conversation developed into a friendly debate about the "moral of the story." We were surprised that there were so many opinions about what the book was trying to say. One student thought the book showed that women can come out ahead in life. Another said the book really showed that, to do well in the United States, you must learn English. One very young woman shook her head and said, "Life is so sad."

This last answer puzzled us, because we wrote the book to have a very positive, upbeat ending. We asked why she said that, and she said, "She and her husband split up and now Betina doesn't have a family with a mother and a father." When another student suggested that maybe Flor was better off without Ricardo, she said, "But Betina is not better off."

When we talked about this later, we realized that these varied reactions were a good indication that the book club was accomplishing exactly what we had hoped. Each student read the story and came up with the theme that meant the most to him or her. The students used a variety of comprehension strategies, from Text-to-Self to Questions and Inferences to talk about the book. The student who said you had to learn English to get ahead wanted a better job and was taking our class so that she could apply for one. The young woman who said life was sad had only seen her father twice. Her mom raised her and her brother. Each of them identified with the book and talked about it in personal ways.

8

Wondering: Questions and Inferences

Prompts: I wonder why. . . .
I wonder how. . . .
I wonder about. . . .
I wonder what the author meant by . . . ?

QUESTIONING the text before, during, and after reading helps students clarify the story's theme, enhances understanding, and propels them though the story. There are major differences between the two questions: *Did Ricardo leave his child?* and *How could Ricardo leave his child?* The answer to the first question is Yes, he did. If a student answers No, he or she obviously has not understood Chapter 1 of *Flor*. However, the answer to the second question is not clear. The answer can be multifaceted, and the reader might need to make that evaluation after reading the whole story. It is a question the reader must ponder, and one that keeps the reader reading. This is what we call an **authentic question,** as opposed to a comprehension question.

One way to make this distinction for the students is to talk about close-ended and open-ended questions. Close-ended questions most often are answered with facts in the text and Yes and No answers. Open-ended questions, on the other hand, do not have pat answers and therefore become great sources of discussion.

Figure 9: Questions and Inferences

We encourage our students to ask these types of questions. We make the distinction between questions that clarify or reveal basic understanding and authentic questions. The first question, *Did Ricardo leave his child?* is a What happened? question. It is useful for understanding the events, but it does not generate discussion. The second is an *I wonder* question. It requires use of background knowledge and inferences about characters and the story to answer. It can engender a lively, opinionated debate.

We want the questions to come from the students, just as we want all the other comprehension strategies to help students express their own ideas and thoughts. Therefore, after the initial modeling, we might record students' questions, but we do not provide lists of questions for them to answer. Our students already have loads of questions (Keene and Zimmerman 1997). We help them articulate their questions (using good English grammar), but we want the questions to be their own.

Questions Using *The Runaway Bunny*

In *The Runaway Bunny* by Margaret Wise Brown, the little bunny insists that he is going to run away from home. An authentic question for this book could be: *I wonder why the little bunny wants to run away from home?* Answers will vary and often lead to Text-to-Self or Text-to-Text connections as well. As an answer to this question, we suggest that the bunny is testing his limits, which leads to anecdotes about our students' childhoods or their children (Text-to-Self), and eventually about parenting skills (Text-to-World).

A student in our class initiated a discussion about how much attention children need and told of her own unhappy childhood, during which she and her siblings were left by their parents to fend for themselves. Another student asked, "I wonder if all children want to run away sometime?" She told of the time that her small child was unhappy with her and wanted to run away, so she helped him pack a bag! By the time the bag was packed, he no longer wanted to go.

Questions Using Other Children's Books

Books with a definite story are best for developing authentic questions (poetry also works well, especially for advanced students). Here are some of our favorites with some examples of wondering type questions.

- ◊ *The Little Mouse, the Red Ripe Strawberry and THE BIG HUNGRY BEAR* by Don and Audrey Wood.
  A little mouse discovers a red ripe strawberry. Someone—we never know who—convinces him that a big hungry bear will get it if the mouse doesn't cut it in half and share it with him.
  Questions: Who is talking to the mouse? I wonder whether the bear really exists. I wonder why the person wants to scare the little mouse.
- ◊ *Miss Nelson Is Missing!* by Harry Allard
  Miss Nelson's class will not behave, and Miss Nelson gets a substitute, Miss Viola Swamp, to whip them into shape.
  Questions: I wonder if Miss Nelson and Miss Swamp are the same person. I wonder why Miss Nelson thought she needed a mean substitute. (This book also can generate an interesting discussion on educational differences in many cultures.)
- ◊ *Pink and Say* by Patricia Polacco
  This is the true story of a young white soldier who was injured in the Civil War and the young black soldier who came to his rescue. At great risk to his mother, the black soldier took the wounded soldier home to her for care.
  Questions: I wonder why Pink rescued Say in the first place. I wonder if Pink really knew how Say felt about the

> war. I wonder why the Confederate soldiers killed Pink's mother. (We have used this book as a prelude to discussions of slavery, the Civil War, civil rights, and Martin Luther King Day. The nature of kindness is an important theme as well.)

As mentioned earlier (see p. viii) fairy tales are also very good for initiating authentic questions. For example, I wonder why Little Red Riding Hood disobeyed her mother. Why didn't she take her warnings seriously? Because fairy tales often have a moral or a lesson, conversations generated by questions can move far beyond the story.

Questions and Inferences using *The Giver*

Lois Lowry's *The Giver* (Reading level grades 5–9) is the story of an ideal future society where there is no pain, no crime, no lying, no uncertainty or unpleasantness, and no memories of the pain and pleasure of life. One man, the Giver, holds all the community's memories, and one boy, Jonas, is specially selected to receive them from the Giver.

In Chapter 8, Jonas learns, in a special ceremony assigning 12-year-olds to the professions in which they will be trained and spend their lives, that he is to be the Receiver. To accept his role, Jonas is asked if he thinks he has the Capacity to See Beyond, which is essential to become a Receiver.

So, a good question for modeling questions might be: *What do you think the Capacity is?* Several clues are presented before Chapter 8 that Jonas is experiencing something strange that he cannot quite describe. For example, he tosses an apple to a friend and the apple changes in a way only he can see. Then in Chapter 8, Jonas sees the whole crowd at the special ceremony change. Great value is placed on being part of the group, fitting in, so Jonas is uncomfortable with the changes he observes. A good whole-class discussion can ensue, using inferences and evidence from the book, as to what the Capacity is. (It turns out that it is the ability to see color; everything in this perfect world is a shade of gray.)

The Giver is a thought-provoking and exciting story of discovery. Themes that can be explored include conforming for the good of society, the value of individualism, and whether suffering is necessary to appreciate pleasure.

Questions Using *Flor*

Throughout *Flor* our students wonder about the relationship between Ricardo and Flor. They lived together as man and wife for several years and had a child, and yet Ricardo left Flor after she had been visiting her family in Mexico for only three months. In an early group discussion about this, one student had a wonderful question: "I wonder if Ricardo always had two families?"

We wrote down this question and looked for the answer as we read the remainder of the book, but we never found it. It is not clear whether Ricardo met a woman with children before Flor left for Mexico, whether he supported two households the entire time he was "married" to Flor, or even whether the children of his other family were his. We talked about this question many times. Some students thought his "new" family must not be so new, and that he wouldn't leave Betina, his daughter, unless he had other children of his own. Others thought Ricardo was just a bad man, and that he was trying to shirk the responsibility for Betina. In all the answers, students had to make inferences about things like Ricardo's motivations, his emotional ties to his children, and his character.

The question's authenticity was confirmed over and over, as we continued to come back to this subject. In the end, Ricardo does provide some monetary support for Betina, as well as wanting to see her every week. Nevertheless, the question, though hotly debated, has no definite answer.

Other questions that have come up in our class and can be used for modeling this strategy are: I wonder why Flor does not get angrier with Ricardo? I wonder why Flor does not return to Mexico? Is Ricardo a bad man? Why did Ricardo take all the furniture when he left?

Questions and inferences are at the center of this book club's discussion.

Photo by Ben Colman.

Troubleshooting

It is especially difficult to model this comprehension strategy with beginning-level students, even using children's books. Their English proficiency is at a concrete, rather than an abstract, level. It could be unsettling to some students not to know the answer. Focusing on other strategies until these students progress to a higher level would be a good idea in this situation. However, using the concrete anger example mentioned in Chapter 6 can help less proficient English students get an idea of what inferring is.

In using *Flor* to model questions, we had to be very clear in our minds whether a question was a comprehension question or an authentic question. We know what happens in the whole book, so a factual question to us could be an authentic question for the students, and they could have a good discussion. There are many instances when the question is unknown to us as well, and that is fun, because we can legitimately enter into the conversation as peers.

9

The Book Log

TO help us remember what has transpired in the book club from week to week, we keep a class Book Log. When we model each comprehension strategy, we do the writing, usually starting on the board and then transferring it to the Book Log. After students form groups, we give the log to each group as they finish their discussions, and they agree on a few sentences to include. In the log we briefly record whole-class discussions and group conversations, and we periodically review with the class what students have written.

As the teachers, we always read the groups' Book Log entries. They help us determine whether our students understand the strategies and how they are progressing in the book. In addition, Book Log entries can be used to assess and address students' writing skills.

We used to keep only one class Book Log, but because groups often hurried through their entries if they thought another group was waiting for the log, we realized we should have two or three. This evolved into having a loose-leaf binder. Then each group can have a separate Book Log sheet with this information printed at the top.

Date: ______________________________
Comprehension Strategy: ______________________________
Title/Chapter: ______________________________
Author: ______________________________
Illustrator: ______________________________
Group Members: ______________________________

Another alternative to a class log is to have students keep their own logs. These logs can be kept in class, or kept by students and brought in on book club day. We have tried both, but we prefer a class log.

After the discussion, students agree on a few lines to describe it. Either one person records for the whole group, or each student writes a sentence or two. Our advanced groups seem to prefer the latter, while our beginning and intermediate groups like having one person write. Sometimes, if there is not enough time to make a Book Log entry, we teachers write down what was discussed so that the ideas are not lost.

Book Log Entry for a Children's Book

Date: 10/15/04
Comprehension Strategy: Summary
Title: The Very Hungry Caterpillar
Author: Eric Carle
Group: Whole morning class
The very hungry caterpillar eats something every day and finally turns into a butterfly.

Book Log Entry Using *Flor*

Date: 4/22/05
Comprehension Strategy: Text-to-Self
Title/Chapter: Flor's Journey to Independence, Ch. 6
Authors: Barbara Vaille and Jennifer QuinnWilliams
Group: P, M, O, H, J
M related to Flor's feeling nervous about telling Lena that she found someone else to watch Betina. In Iran, M was promised a job if she passed a test and even signed an agreement. Then, after she studied hard and passed the exam, the man in charge said she could not have the job after all and he gave it to his son. M was very angry but also very nervous about telling her parents. When she did, they were supportive of her but didn't like the outcome, just as Lena was supportive of Flor even though she didn't like the outcome.

When P came to Denver he couldn't rent an apartment, not because he didn't have the money, like Flor, but because he didn't have any credit. So he worked for six months to establish credit and rented an apartment. Now he has credit cards and everything.

Appendix A provides more examples of Book Log pages that our students have written.

Final Thoughts

AFTER four years of teaching and holding the book club, we have turned some of our students, but not all of them, into independent English readers. Our book club format is simple, but it is not always easy. Some students just want to read the synopsis/summary, and that is enough. Others want to read ahead, but when their out-of-school lives leave little time, they get discouraged. It is an uphill battle to counteract the many outside influences, from busy days to cultural conflicts, to the desire for instant language fixes.

The longer we run the book club, the more adaptable to our students we become. When we have a class of more advanced English speakers and readers, they can run their own book club, from the discussion to the Book Log, with very little assistance from us. This allows us to spend more time with the less proficient students and is actually a great leveling technique in our multilevel class. Some years we run out of time and barely finish reading *Flor* before the year is up. We encourage the students to take home chapters and read like mad. The modified version can be used then, or those who have read the entire book can summarize for the others.

The comprehension strategies enhance our students' understanding of the books they are reading in English. This, in turn, improves their English, which is our main goal: to help our students acquire English.

When our students say they like a book, we feel not only gratified, but we have a sense that it has meaning in their lives. When we are talking about a life skill, and a student interjects with a comparison to *Flor*, we know that he or she is making connections, in English, on a deeper level. And, when one of our Spanish-speaking students struggles excitedly to make her Mongolian group member understand her meaning, finally engaging all six students in the effort, we have the satisfaction of knowing that if they have something they feel is important to express, they will find a way to say it.

We want to plant the seed of lifelong reading and are experiencing the benefits and pleasure of the written word. We will keep at it. It is worth the effort.

Appendix A
Sample Book Log Pages

Date Feb 24, 2003

Comprehension Strategy Predictions

Book Title Flor's Journey to Independence

Author Barbara Vaille and Jennifer QuinnWilliams

Illustrator

Group Members H, M, Y, Y, T, H

Prediction

T: I think Flor will be work in Burger King yet, but may be later she will find better job. I think Flor will pick up her daughter from her mother-in-law and Carmen will be take care about Betina. I think Ricardo will not come back to Flor and Flor will not care about it, and she will meet nice man someday.

H: I think Flor will be sick. Because she works hard every day and she is busy. But finally Ricardo will come back her and Betina.

Y: I think this all story Flor's dream. Flors get up on the bus. They get down from the bus. Ricardo pic up them. HAPPY END! I hope.

H: Flor will work hard to live herself with Betina. Ricardo will visit her and regret he did something wrong. But Flor isn't going to forgive him. She can live by herself, and in the future, she will find a right person.

Y: Flor will find new job and she can get enough money. She will be moved to new house with Betina.

M: I think, Flor is going to buy one little gun and every day she is looking for Ricardo! She tried to find him, but Ricardo doesn't appear. She will go to Mexico with her daughter, after to kill her husband.

Date 3/10/2003

Comprehension Strategy Questions

Book Title Flor's Journey to Independence

Author Barbara Vaille and Jennifer QuinnWilliams

Illustrator

Group Members Y, H, Y, B, M, and M

Questions

Why don't Flor and Betina go back to Mexico?

Why doesn't Ricardo pay more money?

Is Ricardo Mexican or American?

Why did Flor and Betina go back to Mexico for 3 month (so long time)?

When did Ricardo make other girlfriend?

Why is Maria so angry?

Date 2/07/04
Comprehension Strategy Summary
Book Title Flor's Journey to Independence, modified Ch. 1
Author Barbara Vaille and Jennifer QuinnWilliams
Illustrator
Group Members Q, J, G

Who is in the story?

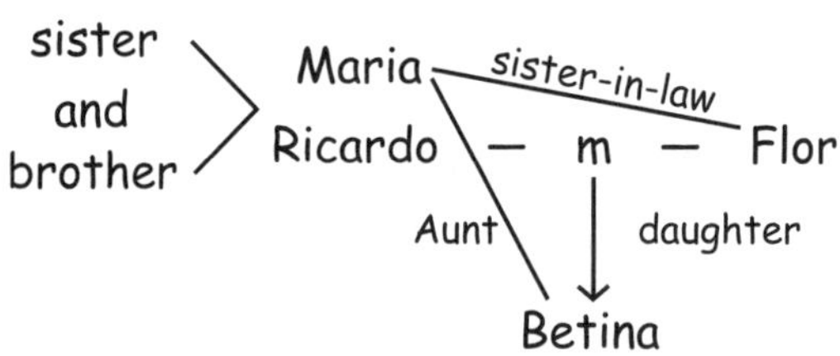

What happens in the story?

Flor and Betina had a vacation in Mexico and Flor lost her husband. He cheated on her.

How long did they stay in Mexico?

3 months

Date September 24, 2004

Comprehension Strategy Text-to-Self

Book title Flor's Journey to Independence

Author Barbara and Jennifer

Illustrator

Group Members E, R, M, and M

R: This is phrase "She felt like she was under water" reminds me a bad sitation I lived: I was working in a hospital. I had a pain in my shoulders. The manager tried cach me making small mistakes and I felt like "was under water".

E: My husband had the same situation with her husband. And for me is sad untill now.

M: Burger King manager "He spoke Spanish" The phrase remnds me first job application. I went japanese restaurant owner was japanese. I was in luck. I got job right away.

M: This history is very sad for me because reminds me a situation in my family and in my life. The men from Mexico have two wives in the same time but they think that is no bad for them, but for the women is very bad. Ricardo thinks he is right taking other wife and he doesn't think about Betina feelings.

Date 4/4/03
Comprehension Strategy Text-to-Self
Book title Suppertime for Frieda Fuzzypaws
Author Cyndy Szekeres
Group Members M, C, L

M: Remember when I boy, my Mama I to seat in table eating food soup and dondt not cookees yes

C: My daughter no likes tha pasta eggs rice she likes hambugs burritos chees tha frut

L: MY BEBI NO LIKE EN DE BINS EN RAYS – YES LAKED KANDIS

Date: October 21, 2004
Comprehension Strategy Text-to-Text, Text-to-Self
Book Title Help!
Author Philip Prowse
Illustrator Gary Taylor
Group Members M, D, and M

M: this book reminds me that I saw a story about an author who has a little plant who help to him to write. He needed to say the tittle of the story and the little plant writes the story in the typing machine. He was very happy because he doesn't write and he got a lot of money. But one day the plant dead and he was very sad.

M: this book reminds me when I learned the computer at the first time. Actually, I don't like to handle a machine...But my husband advised to learn the computer. As I know more and more about computer, Like this book's Wormold, I am getting happier. Maybe I guess we (I and Wormold) had similar feeling and experience.

D: This story reminds me something about Text-to-Self. Two things are importants on the book. Frank is a writer and I like to write, and Frank use a computers, I like the computers.

Date 12/13/04

Comprehension Strategy All

Book title Too Many Tamales

Author Gary Soto

Illustrator

Group Members Whole-class discussion

Whole class was very interested in picture of the father in an apron, cooking.

M: In your country do men go into the kitchen for cooking?

M: Do Mexican men help in the kitchen? My image is that the story is not common. Is this what men do when the family makes tamales?

M: Its not so common the men help.

J: when my mother went back to work my father learned to cook. We divided up the tasks in the kitchen and we all helped.

M: Every day I make a recipe for my daughter. She very exciting about her cookbook.

L: My mother never taught me to cook. I had four brothers and me only girl. She said, "Go with your brothers." My grandmother said, "She never get married!" In here, I learn to cook. First year, my husband cook. Now, when I cook, he says, "Delicious!"

Date 3/17/04

Comprehension Strategy All

Book title Flor's Journey to Independence

Author Barbara Vaille and Jennifer QuinnWilliams

Illustrator

Group Members N, J, M, R, W, A

W: Prediction—Betina will die. She is unconscious and many bad things happen to Flor.

R: Text-to-Self—When he first came here many people told him that he needed to get a woman, even though he had a wife and three children in Mexico. He suffered a lot.

N: Text-to-World—Similar situation in Mongolia when women don't have husbands, they have a hard time.

A: Life is not easy. Here and there there are problems always.

J: Text-to-Self—He had a hard time when he first came and didn't know English.

M: Text-to-World—Many problems for wrong beliefs. In Mexcio when people live together, the man takes all the furniture and the woman has nothing. Man has kids, everything.

Appendix B
Resources and Texts for Intermediate to More Advanced Readers

Note: Although most of the books listed are for older children (middle-schoolers and above), with the exception of some of the books in the series listed, we have read and enjoyed them all. See note regarding fairy tales on page 109.

Websites

www.ala.org. To find lists of award-winning books, including winners of the Caldecott Medal, Newbery Medal, and Belpré Medal (outstanding children's literature that celebrates the Latino experience), and the Alex Awards (ten best adult books that appeal to young adults), click on Awards and Scholarships, then on Book/Media Awards. The winners and honorable mentions are listed and summarized. Also features Book List Magazine online, a very good source for high-quality fiction and non-fiction books for all ages on all topics.

www.classicreader.com. Hundreds of books and stories in the public domain, so they can be copied. You can search by fiction, non-fiction, drama, and more. No plot summaries; you have to know what you're looking for.

www.hornbookguide.com. Reviews of every hardcover trade book published in the United States for young people. Subscription service.

www.nancykeane.com. The Booktalks section has lists of books with informative summaries for young to middle school children, and some teen books. It includes a subject list, an author list, and good links to other sources.

www.sbfonline.com. Science biographies.

www.education-world.com. Lists of top middle school books and links to other review sites.

Fiction

Alvarez, J. *Before We Were Free*. New York: Knopf, 2002.
Told through the eyes of a 12-year-old girl, the story of a family struggling for freedom under a dictatorship (Dominican Republic). Reading level young adult (grade 9+)

Anaya, R. *Bless Me Ultima*. New York: Warner Books, 1994.
A Chicano boy travels to rural New Mexico with a curandera. Reading level all ages

Becker, M. *Samantha*. Ann Arbor: University of Michigan Press, 1993.

———. *Samantha: The Sequel*. Ann Arbor: University of Michigan Press, 2000.
A two-part soap opera about Samantha and the relationships in her life.

Collier, J., and C. Collier. *My Brother Sam Is Dead*. New York: Scholastic, 1985.
A revolutionary war story about divided loyalties. Reading level young adult (grade 9+)

Cormier, R. *The Chocolate War*. New York: Laurel Leaf, 1986.
A portrait of cruelty and conformity in an exclusive prep school. Reading level grades 9–12

Creech, S. *Love that Dog*. New York: Harper Trophy, 2003.
A young student, who comes to love poetry through a personal understanding of what different famous poems mean to him, surprises himself by writing his own inspired poem. Reading level grades 4–6

Donnelly, J. *A Northern Light*. New York: Harcourt, 2003.
A young woman, in love with words, has a dream of attending college. Set in 1906 rural New York state. Reading level grades 9–12

Farmer, N. *The House of the Scorpion.* New York: Atheneum Books for Young Readers, 2002.
A futuristic tale of clones and a new country formed between the United States and Mexico, called Opium. A young clone seeks the secret of his existence and eventually finds reserves of wisdom and courage. Reading level grades 5–9

Frost, H. *Keesha's House.* New York: Farrar, Straus & Giroux, 2003.
Teenage Keesha runs a house for other kids having hard times with their families. Reading level young adult (grade 9+)

Glass, Julia. *Three Junes.* New York: Anchor Books, 2003.
Taking place during three separate summers, this novel examines one family's secrets and ties through the stories of three of its members. Reading level adult

Goldman, W. *The Princess Bride.* New York: Ballantine Books, 1998.
A comic adventure romance full of swashbuckling action. Reading level grades 4–6

Hesse, K. *Out of the Dust.* New York: Scholastic, 1999.
First-person free-verse poetry. The story of Billie Jo's courage in enduring her mother's death, for which she is blamed, her father's decline into alcoholism, and life during the Great Depression.

Lowry, L. *The Giver.* New York: Laurel Leaf, 2002.
In a colorless but safe community, the residents only have memories of their generation. What happens when the keeper of the memories (the Giver) and the chosen memory recipient (the Receiver) decide to change this way of life? Newbery Medal winner. Reading level grades 5–9

Nesbit, W. *The Railway Children.* Oxford: Oxford University Press, 2000.
When their father mysteriously disappears, three English children move with their mother to a small house near a railway line. Reading level grades 3–6

Prowse, P. *Help.* Cambridge: Cambridge University Press, 1999.
A level 1 book written for adult English learners. A comic tale in which Frank Wormwold's computer gives him more help than he wants with his book.

Ryan, P. M. *Esperanza Rising.* New York: Blue Sky Press, 2002.
A Depression-era story of a rich young girl whose family loses everything. Esperanza finds something else, though, as she grows to womanhood. Belpré Medal winner. Reading level grades 3–6

Sachar, L. *Holes.* New York: Farrar, Strauss & Giroux, 1998.
Sent to a desert camp for a crime he didn't commit (stealing some famous tennis shoes), the protagonist discovers courage, creativity, and friendship in a slightly askew world. Very funny, but suspenseful. Newbery Medal winner. Reading level grades 4–6

Testa, M. *Becoming Joe DiMaggio.* Cambridge, MA: Candlewick Press, 2002.
Poetry. A fatherless boy's story about life, family, and baseball. Reading level grades 4–7

Non-Fiction and Non-Fiction Series

Angelou, M. *I Know Why the Caged Bird Sings.* New York: Bantam, 1983.
An emotionally difficult but ultimately uplifting autobiography of Maya Angelou, the writer and poet. Reading level young adult (grade 9+)

Frank, A. *Anne Frank: The Diary of a Young Girl.* New York: Bantam, 1993.
Classic tale of a courageous, creative young Jewish girl and her family hiding out from the Nazis in Amsterdam. Reading level all ages

Green, M. *A Strong Right Arm.* New York: Dial Books for Young Readers, 2002.
Biography of Mamie "Peanut" Johnson, one of only three women to play in the Negro Baseball League. Reading level grades 4–7

The Importance of . . . Stamford, CT: Lucent Books, 1994ff. (Series)
A series of biographies of famous celebrities, politicians, scientists, etc., from around the world. Reading level grades 4–7

Jimenez, F. *The Circuit: Stories from the Life of a Migrant Child.* Albuquerque, NM: University of New Mexico Press, 1997.
Stories based on the author's own life as the child of migrant farm workers. Reading level grades 4–8

———. *Breaking Through.* Boston: Houghton-Mifflin, 2002.
Sequel to *The Circuit*; covers the author's life, through teen years and college. Reading level grades 5–8

Krull, K. *Lives of...* San Diego: Harcourt Children's Books. (Series)
Stories of famous people (extraordinary women, presidents, athletes, artists, writers, musicians) with a twist, focusing on their achievements and their quirks. Reading level grades 4–8

People at the Center of . . . Farmington Hills, MI: Blackbirch Press (Series)
Biographies of noteworthy individuals from history. Reading level grades 5–9

Unblocking the Secrets of Science. Newark, DE: Mitchell Lane Publishers (Series)
Biographies of scientists and their discoveries in interesting story format, organized into Inventors, Scientists, and Pioneers. Reading level grades 5–9

Appendix C Additional Children's Literature

Fiction

<u>Note</u>: All of the children's books are written for ages 4–8, or Reading level grades 1–3, but some are simpler than others.

Bloom, B. *Wolf!* New York: Scholastic, 1999.
Surrounded by educated animals, a wolf thinks that maybe he could learn to read.

Bunting, E. *Butterfly House.* New York: Scholastic, 1999.
With the help of her grandfather, a little girl makes a house for a larva and watches it develop before setting it free. Every spring after that butterflies come to visit her.

Carle, E. *The Grouchy Ladybug.* New York: HarperCollins, 1996.
A grouchy ladybug, looking for a fight, challenges everyone she meets, regardless of their size or strength.

Carlson, N. *I Like Me!* New York: Penguin Putnum Books for Young Readers, 1990.
By admiring her finer points and proving you can have fun even when no one else is around, a charming pig proves the best friend you can have is yourself.

Cowley, J. *Hungry Monster.* Washington: The Wright Group, 1990.
A hungry monster goes looking for breakfast and eats some surprising things.

———. *The Monsters' Party.* Washington: The Wright Group, 1990.
Several little monsters wonder what they can do at a party.

———. *Who Will Be My Mother?* Washington: The Wright Group, 1990.
After a little lamb's mother dies, she asks all the animals if they will take her place.

Creech, S. *A Fine, Fine School*. New York: Joanna Cotler Books, 2001.
What happens when an over-zealous principal takes the love of learning too far and requires school on Saturday?

dePaola, T. *Nana Downstairs & Nana Upstairs*. New York: Putnam, 2000.
Four-year-old Tommy enjoys his relationships with both his grandmother and his great-grandmother, but eventually must learn to face their inevitable deaths.

———. *Tony's Bread: An Italian Folktale*. New York: Putnam, 1989.
A baker loses his daughter but gains a bakery in the grand city of Milano after meeting a determined nobleman and baking a unique loaf of bread.

Ehlert, L. *Growing Vegetable Soup*. New York: Scholastic, 1987.
A child tells about the process of growing vegetables, from seeds to soup.

Escott, J. *Hannah and the Hurricane*. White Plains, NY: Pearson, 1998.
An Easystart book with 200 words, all in present tense. A morality tale in which Hannah saves a greedy tour-boat operator from a hurricane, changing his attitude through her bravery.

Ets, M. H. *Gilberto and the Wind*. New York: Puffin Books, 1978.
A little boy plays with the wind.

———. 1965. *Just Me*. New York: Puffin Books, 1978.
A little boy mimes the walk of the animals he sees.

Haseley, Dennis. *A Story for Bear*. New York: Silver Whistle Harcourt, Inc., 2002.
A young bear who is fascinated by the mysterious marks he sees on paper finds a friend when a kind woman reads to him.

Hoban, R. *A Baby Sister for Frances*. New York: Harper and Row, 1976.
Upon the birth of her sister, Frances decides to run away. Her parents cleverly remind her of how much she is loved and needed.

Hutchins, P. *The Wind Blew*. New York: Aladdin, 1993.
A rhymed tale describing the antics of the wind.

Johnston, T. *My Mexico-Mexico Mio*. New York: Putnam, 1996.
Poems of common sights in Mexico. In English and Spanish.

Keats, E. J. *The Snowy Day*. New York: Puffin Books, 1962.
A small boy experiences the joy of a snowy day. Caldecott Medal winner.

———. *Whistle for Willie*. New York: Viking, 1964.
A little boy tries and tries to whistle for his dog, Willie.

Krauss, R. *Bears*. New York: HarperCollins, 2005.
This book is filled with funny bears in funny places.

Lionni, L. *A Color of His Own*. Scholastic: New York, 1975.
A chameleon searches for his own color, and on the way discovers an amazing trait he has.

———. *Swimmy*. New York: Knopf, 1973.
A little black fish in the sea saves a school of red fish from the big fish.

Muth, J. J. *The Three Questions*. New York: Scholastic, 2002.
Nikolai asks his animal friends to help him answer three important questions: "When is the best time to do things?" "Who is the most important one?" and "What is the right thing to do?"

Najimy, N. *Hopeless Homer*. New York: SRA/Macmillan/McGraw–Hill, 1995.
A boy at camp can't do anything right until a toad appears which everyone else was afraid of.

Numeroff, L. J. *If You Give a Mouse a Cookie*. New York: HarperCollins, 1995.
Relating the cycle of requests a mouse is likely to make after you give him a cookie takes the reader through a young boy's day.

O'Brien, A. S. *My Name is Johari*. New York: Newbridge Communications, Inc., 1996.
Johari learns how special her name is.

Paulsen, G. *The Tortilla Factory*. Carmel, CA: Hampton Brown, 1995.
The cycle of life from the seeds to corn to tortilla factory to table to farmer to earth and back to seeds.

Polacco, P. *Aunt Chip and the Great Triple Creek Dam Affair.* New York: Philomel Books, 1996.
Aunt Chip saves the town of Triple Creek, where everyone has forgotten how to read because of the invasion of television.

———. *Thank You, Mr. Falker.* New York: Philomel Books, 1998.
At first, Trish loves school, but her difficulty learning to read makes her feel dumb, until, in the fifth grade, a new teacher helps her understand and overcome her problem.

Rylant, C. *In November.* New York: Harcourt, 2000.
Describes the autumn activities and traditions that November's cooling temperatures bring.

———. *The Wonderful Happens.* New York: Simon & Schuster, 2000.
Describes some of the things that bring happiness and awe into our lives.

Sage, A. *Monkeys in the Jungle.* Boston: Houghton Mifflin, 1993.
Monkeys, bats, tigers, and other animals are just waiting for the reader to discover where they are.

Sendak, M. *Where the Wild Things Are.* New York: HarperCollins, 1988.
A little boy dreams of an adventure with monsters.

Shelby, A. *Potluck.* Boston: Houghton Mifflin, 1995.
Kids from around the world bring food to a potluck, everything from A to Z.

Taha, K. T. *A Gift for Tía Rosa.* New York: Bantam, 1991.
An elderly aunt teaches Carmela how to knit and much more. When she dies, Carmela learns how to honor her memory.

Viorst, J. *Alexander and the Terrible, Horrible, No-Good, Very Bad Day.* New York: Scholastic, 1972.
Alexander wakes up to gum in his hair, and it only gets worse.

Waber, B. *Do You See a Mouse?* New York: Houghton Mifflin, 1995.
Everyone at an ultra-fancy hotel insists that there is no mouse in the hotel, but the reader can see a mouse in each illustration.

Waddell, M. *Farmer Duck.* Cambridge, MA: Candlewick Press, 1992.
When a kind and hardworking duck nearly collapses from overwork, the rest of the animals get together and chase the lazy farmer out of town.

Walter, M. *Ty's One-man Band.* New York: Scholastic, 1984.
When a one-legged man comes to town, he shows Ty and everyone else how to make music with common household items.

Ward, L. *I Am Eyes—Ni Macho.* New York: Scholastic, 1988.
Africa is brought to life by all that a little girl sees when she wakes up.

Walsh, E. S. *Mouse Paint.* New York: Harcourt, 1989.
Three white mice discover jars of red, blue, and yellow paint and explore the world of color.

Wild, M., and R. Brooks. *Fox.* La Jolla, CA: Kane/Miller Book Publishers, 2001.
An injured magpie and a one-eyed dog live happily together in the forest, until a jealous fox arrives to teach them what it means to be alone.

Yashima, T. *Crow Boy.* New York: Puffin Books, 1976.
Classmates come to appreciate a country boy and understand him through the efforts of a teacher.

———. *Umbrella.* New York: Puffin Books, 1985.
Momo eagerly waits for a rainy day so she can use the red boots and umbrella she received on her third birthday. Caldecott Honor book.

Fairy Tales

<u>Note</u>: Many fairly tales and fables list no author. These are versions we like because of the way the story is told or because the illustrations are particularly good, or both. They are listed in alphabetical order by title. For versions that can be used with adults, try *Open Sesame: Understanding American English and Culture through Folktales and Stories* by Planaria J. Price (University of Michigan Press, 1997).

Chicken Little. Wisconsin: Golden Press, 1973.
The funny tale of Chicken Little, who convinces the barnyard animals that the sky is falling.

The Emperor's New Clothes. New York: Margaret K. McElderry Books, 2000. (Author: Demi)
Two rascals sell a Chinese emperor an invisible set of clothes.

Henny Penny. New York: Clarion Books, 1968. (Author: Paul Galdone)
Another version of the famous "The sky is falling!" story.

Jack and the Beanstalk. New York: Clarion Books, 1974. (Author: Paul Galdone)
A different version of the story of the magic bean, told in rhyme. There's no gold involved, but Jack gets to marry the Giant's maid.

The Little Red Hen. New York: Random House, 1982.
A Little Golden Book version of the industrious hen and her lazy friends who won't help her work, but want to share the rewards.

Little Red Riding Hood. New York: Scholastic, 1986.
The pretty illustrations in this story of the little girl fooled by the wolf in the forest make this a good read-aloud tale.

Red Riding Hood. New York: Dial Books for Young Readers, 1987. (Author: James Marshall)
The very funny illustrations and dialogue in this version of the little girl led astray by a hungry wolf freshen the tale.

Non-Fiction

Ancona, G. *The Piñata Maker*. Orlando, FLA: Harcourt, 1994.
Describes how Don Ricardo, a craftsman from Elutia de Crespa in southern Mexico, makes piñatas for all the village birthday parties and other fiestas.

Bailey, D. *Where We Live: Mexico*. Austin, TX: Steck-Vaughn, 1990.
Depicts the occupations, daily activities, festivals, and ceremonies of Mexico.

Maestro B. *The Story of the Statue of Liberty.* New York: Lothrop, Lee & Shepard Books, 1986.
Describes the creation of the huge statue given by France to the United States and its erection in New York Harbor as a symbol of liberty.

Martin, J. B. *Snowflake Bentley.* Boston: Houghton Mifflin, 1998.
A biography of a self-taught scientist who photographed thousands of individual snowflakes in order to study their unique formations. Caldecott Medal winner.

Marzollo, J. *Happy Birthday, Martin Luther King.* New York: Scholastic, 1993.
The story of Martin Luther King's life is told, accompanied by beautiful scratchboard and oil pastel illustrations.

McGovern, A. *Wanted, Dead or Alive: The True Story of Harriet Tubman.* New York: Scholastic, 1991.
The true story of Harriet Tubman and how she led hundreds of slaves to freedom on the secret Underground Railroad.

Appendix D
Suggested Time Line

Suggested Time Line for Introducing the Book Club in a Multilevel Class with *Flor* and Children's Books in a One-Hour Class (3 times per week)

Week 1: The Summary	Explain the rationale for reading in class. Explain the concept of the Book Club using the chart (p. 14). Read a children's book and summarize, using The Book-in-Hand.
Week 2: *Flor* summaries Reading: 20–30 minutes Summaries: 30 minutes	**Students read *Flor*, Ch. 1.** Students form groups and summarize, using The Book-in-Hand.
Week 3: Text-to-Self Modeling: 30 minutes Discussion: 20 minutes	Model Text-to-Self using a children's book. Introduce concept of discussion leader. Students form groups, choose a leader, and make Text-to-Self connections from *Flor*, Ch. 1.
Week 4: Text-to-World Modeling: 25 minutes Reading: 20 minutes Discussion: 15 minutes	Model Text-to-World using a children's book or a newspaper clipping. **Students read *Flor*, Ch. 2**, form groups, and make Text-to-World connections.
Week 5: Text-to-Text Modeling: 25 minutes Reading: 20 minutes Text-to-Text: 15 minutes	Model Text-to-Text using two children's books. Students form groups. Each group reads a teacher-selected children's book and makes Text-to-Text connections to one of the books the teacher modeled.
Week 6: Sensory Images Modeling: 30 minutes Reading: 20 minutes Discussion: 10 minutes	Model Sensory Images using pictures. **Students read *Flor*, Ch. 3,** and discuss their images.
Week 7: Predictions and Inferences Modeling: 30 minutes Discussion: 30 minutes	Model Predictions and Inferences using a children's book. Students form groups and make predictions based on *Flor*, Ch. 3.
Week 8: Questions and Inferences Modeling: 30 minutes Discussion: 30 minutes	Model authentic Questions and Inferences using a children's book. Students form groups and make authentic questions from *Flor*, Ch.3.

Note: To save time in a one-hour class, decide on groups before class and put the students in their groups before you model. Then students can read (to themselves) while in their groups and don't need to rearrange themselves for the discussion. Check for understanding during the book club discussions, and assist any groups that are having trouble. If you want to do a Book Log, wait until you've taught all the comprehension strategies, and then take 20 minutes or so of the next book club class to explain it.

Book Club Format

1. Select one person to SUMMARIZE for the other group(s).
   - ☐ A-Book-in-Hand
   - ☐ Who? What? Where? When? Why? How?
2. Select a DISCUSSION LEADER. (Optional)
3. Pick a COMPREHENSION STRATEGY to guide your discussion.
   Text-to-Self (personal connections, personal opinions)
   Prompts: "This reminds me of my. . . ." "This reminds me of the time I. . . ." "I think. . . ."
   Queries: How was it the same? How was it different? What would you do if . . .?
   Text-to-World (world connections, cultural connections)
   Prompts: "This reminds me of. . . ." "In my country. . . ."
   Queries: How was it the same? How was it different?
   Text-to-Text (connections to other books, articles, movies)
   Prompts: "I read a book (saw a movie, etc.) like this. . . ."
   Queries: How was it the same? How was it different?
   Sensory Images (what you see, hear, smell, etc. in your mind as you read)
   Prompts: "I see (smell, hear, taste). . . ." "I think (character) is. . . ."
   Queries: "What does (character) look like?" "What do you see in this chapter?"
   "What does it (sound, taste, feel, smell) like?"
   Predictions and Inferences (based on what you know, make a guess)
   Prompts: "I think . . . will happen because. . . ."
   Queries: What do you think will happen to . . .? What do you think will happen next? Why?
   Questions and Inferences (Authentic versus comprehension questions)
   "What does . . . mean?" "What did the author mean by . . .?" "I wonder why . . . ." "I wonder how. . . ." "I wonder about. . . ."
4. Read the selection. (If you read at home, go on to 5.)
5. Discuss the selections and your reactions and connections. Remember to follow up!
6. Record/write in the Book Log.
7. Summarize your selection for the other group(s).

This page is reproducible. Copyright © 2006 The University of Michigan.

Bibliography

Professional Resources

Anderson, R. C., P. T. Wilson, and L. G. Fielding. "Growth in Reading and How Children Spend Their Time Outside of School." *Reading Research Quarterly* 23 (1988): 285–303.

Bloom, B. S. *Taxonomy of Educational Objectives: The Classification of Educational Goals: Handbook I Cognitive Domain*. New York: Longman, 1956.

Brock, C. "Exploring the Use of Book Club with Second Language Learners in the Mainstream Classroom," 141–61. In *The Book Club Connection: Literacy Learning and Classroom Talk,* ed. S. I. McMahon, T. E. Raphael, V. Goatley, and L. S. Pardo. New York: Teachers College Press, 1997.

Brock, C. "Organizing Literature-Based Reading Instruction for Second Language Learners." Paper presented at the International Reading Association Annual Conference, Anaheim, CA, 1995.

Cho, K., and S. Krashen. "Acquisition of Vocabulary" from *Sweet Valley Kids* Series, Adult ELL Acquisition. *Journal of Reading* 37, no. 8 (1994): 662–67.

Cuban, S. "Reading for Pleasure." *Focus on Basics* 5 (2001): 20–23.

Daniels, H. *Literature Circles: Voice and Choice in the Student-Centered Classroom.* York, ME: Stenhouse Publishers, 1994.

Dulay, H., M. Burt, and S. Krashen. *Language Two.* New York: Oxford University Press, 1982.

Elley, R. *Raising Literacy Levels in Third World Countries: A Method that Works.* Culver City, CA: Language Education Associates, 1998.

Elley, W., and F. Mangubhai. "The Impact of Reading on Second Language Learning." *Reading Research Quarterly* 19 (1983): 53–67.

Foertsch, M. *Reading In and Out of School.* Washington, DC: U.S. Department of Education, 1992.

Goatley, V. J., C. Brock, and T. E. Raphael. "Diverse Learners Participating in Regular Education Book Clubs." *Reading Research Quarterly* 30, no. 3 (1995): 352–80.

Gradman, H., and E. Hanania. "The Relative Importance of Reading for Language Learning Programs." In *QUILT and QUILL: Achieving and Maintaining Quality in Teaching and Learning.* Hong Kong: Dept. of Language Education, 1991.

Graves, D. *Build a Literate Classroom.* Portsmouth, NH: Heinemann, 1991.

Harvey, S., and A. Goudvis. *Strategies that Work: Teaching Comprehension to Enhance Understanding.* York, ME: Stenhouse Publishers, 2000.

Keene, E., and S. Zimmerman. *Mosaic of Thought: Teaching Comprehension in a Reader's Workshop.* Portsmouth, NH: Heinemann, 1997.

Krashen, S. *Explorations in Language Acquisition and Use.* Portsmouth, NH: Heinemann, 2003.

———. *The Power of Reading: Insights from the Research.* Englewood, CO: Libraries Unlimited Inc., 1993.

Lao, C. Y., and S. Krashen. "The Impact of Popular Literature Study on Literary Development in EFL: More Evidence for the Power of Reading." *System* 28 (2000): 261–70.

Mason, B., and S. Krashen. "Extensive Reading in English as a Foreign Language." *System* 25 (1997): 91–102.

McMahon, S. I., T. E. Raphael, V. Goatley, and L. S. Pardo. *The Book Club Connection: Literacy Learning and Classroom Talk.* New York: Teacher's College Press, 1997.

Nagy, W., P. Herman, and R. Anderson. "Learning Words from Context." *Reading Research Quarterly* 20: (1985): 233–53.

Raphael, T. E., and C. Brock. "Mei: Learning the Literacy Culture in an Urban Elementary School." In *Examining Central Issues in Literacy Research, Theory and Practice,* eds. D. Leu and C. Kinzer, 179–89. Chicago: National Reading Conference, 1993.

Seabright, W. *An Introduction to Shared Inquiry*. Chicago: The Great Books Foundation, 1992.

Trelease, J. *The Read-Aloud Handbook. 5th ed.* New York: Penguin, 2001.

U.S. Department of Education. *Focus on Basics*. National Center for the Study of Adult Learning and Literacy.

VanPatten, B. *From Input to Output: A Teacher's Guide to Second Language Acquisition*. New York: McGraw Hill, 2002.

Zimmerman, S., and C. Hutchins. *7 Keys to Comprehension: How to Help Your Kids Read and Get It!* New York: Three Rivers Press, 2003.

Children's Fiction

Aardema, V. *Bringing the Rain to Kapiti Plain*. New York: Dial Books for Young Readers, 1983.

———. *Why Mosquitos Buzz in People's Ears*. Richmond, VA: Time Life Books, 1975.

Allard, H. *Miss Nelson Is Missing!* Boston: Houghton Mifflin, 1977.

Baker, J. *Where the Forest Meets the Sea*. New York: Greenwillow Books, 1987.

Brown, M. W. 1947. *Goodnight Moon*. New York: HarperTrophy, 1977.

———. *The Runaway Bunny*. New York: HarperFestival, 1991.

Carle, E. *The Very Hungry Caterpillar*. New York: Philomel Books, 1969.

Cowley, J. *Turnips for Dinner*. New York: Modern Publishing, 1986.

d'A Sales, F. *Ibrahim*. Philadelphia: Lippincott, 1989.

Fox, M. *Guess What?* Orlando, FL: Harcourt, 1988.

Jacobs, A. J. *Fractured Fairy Tales*. New York: Bantam, 1997.

Joosse, B. M. *Mama, Do You Love Me?* San Francisco: Chronicle Books, 1991.

Kraus, R. *Where Are You Going, Little Mouse?* New York: HarperTrophy, 1989.

———. *Whose Mouse Are You?* New York: Simon and Schuster Children's Publishing, 2000.

Krauss, R. *The Carrot Seed.* New York: HarperTrophy, 1989.

Scieszka, J. *The True Story of the Three Little Pigs.* New York: Puffin Books, 1996.

Soto, G. *Too Many Tamales.* New York: Putnam, 1993.

Steig, W. *Sylvester and the Magic Pebble.* New York: Simon and Schuster Books for Young Readers, 1969.

———. *Suppertime for Frieda Fuzzypaws.* Racine, WI: Western Publishing Company, Inc., 1985.

Titherington, J. *Pumpkin, Pumpkin.* New York: Scholastic, 1986.

Trussel-Cullen, A. *This Is the Plate.* Glenview, IL.: Scott Foresman, 1993.

White, E. B. *Charlotte's Web.* New York: HarperCollins, 1999.

Wild, M. *Fox.* La Jolla, CA: Kane/Miller Book Publishers, 2001.

Williams, L. *The Little Old Lady Who Was Not Afraid of Anything.* New York: HarperTrophy, 1986.

Wood, D., and A. Wood. *The Little Mouse, the Red Ripe Strawberry and THE BIG HUNGRY BEAR.* Singapore: Child's Play International, 1984.

Children's Non-Fiction

Argueta, J. *A Movie in My Pillow.* San Francisco: Children's Book Press, 2001.

Fritz, J. *And Then What Happened, Paul Revere?* New York: Putnam, 1996.

Miller, W. *Frederick Douglass: The Last Day of Slavery.* New York: Lee & Low Books, Inc., 1995.

Polacco, P. *Pink and Say.* New York: Philomel Books, 1994.

For Intermediate to More Advanced Readers

Farley, W. *Man o' War.* New York: Random House, 1962.

Goldman, W. *The Princess Bride.* New York: Ballantine Books, 1973.

Hillenbrand, L. *Seabiscuit: An American Legend.* New York: Random House, 2001.

L'Engle, M. *A Swiftly Tilting Planet.* New York: Farrar, Straus & Giroux, 1978.

———. *A Wind in the Door.* New York: Farrar, Straus & Giroux, 1973.

———. *A Wrinkle in Time.* New York: Farrar, Straus & Giroux, 1962.

Levine, G. *Ella Enchanted.* New York: HarperCollins, 1997.

Lowry, L. *The Giver.* New York: Bantam, Dell, Doubleday Publishing, Inc., 1993.

Speare, Elizabeth G. *The Witch of Blackbird Pond.* New York: Yearling, 1987.

White, E. B. *Charlotte's Web.* New York: HarperCollins, 1999.

Index

Acknowledgments

Grateful acknowledgment is given to the following for permission to reprint their materials.

Corbis for photos of Female Student Reading and Two Young Women Reading a Book. All rights reserved.

Fotosearch, LLC, for photo of Four Students Sitting Outdoors. All rights reserved.

Grateful acknowledgment is also given to Ben Colman, Linda Colman, Gerri Barr, Tom Egle, Judy Dean, and Gretchen Casper.